THE WAR
of
JENKINS'
EAR

The Forgotten Struggle for North and South America:
1739–1742

ROBERT GAUDI

PEGASUS BOOKS
NEW YORK LONDON

THE WAR OF JENKINS' EAR

Pegasus Books, Ltd.
148 West 37th Street, 13th Floor
New York, NY 10018

First Pegasus Books paperback edition October 2022
First Pegasus Books cloth edition November 2021

Interior design by Sheryl P. Kober

ISBN: 978-1-63936-296-7

10 9 8 7 6 5 4 3 2 1

Printed in the United States of America
Distributed by Simon & Schuster
www.pegasusbooks.com

For D.H.W. in gratitude for his many kindnesses.

And for my children, with love.

Historians are dependent on their sources. Had I more time and ability, I should have made this book a novel, for there are so many things the sources do not tell. There are heroisms unrecorded, great moments of beauty and courage that have left no trace, unknowable human experiences that would teach wisdom and understanding . . . The historian can never construct a record of events. All he can do is construct a record of records.

—J.H. POWELL, *BRING OUT YOUR DEAD*, 1949

Our Merchants and ears a strange bother have made,
with Losses sustained in their ships and their trade;
But now they may laugh and quite banish their fears,
Nor mourn for lost Liberty, riches and ears.

—ENGLISH STREET BALLAD, C. 1739.
(Written upon declaration of war against Spain.)

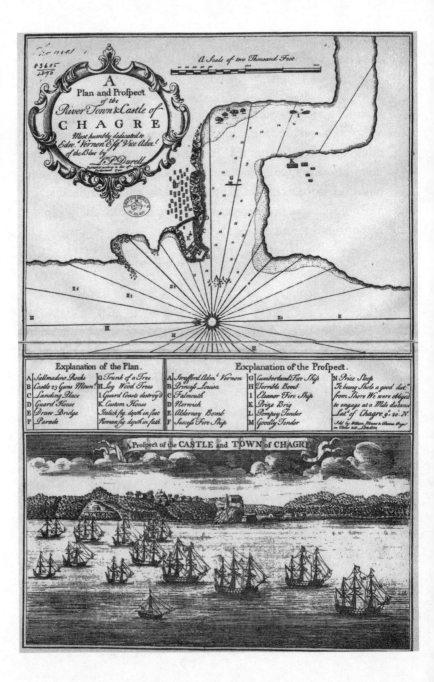

A Scale of two Thousand Feet.

A
Plan and Prospect
of the
River Town & Castle of
CHAGRE
Most humbly dedicated to
Edw.ᵈ Vernon Esq.ʳ Vice Adm.ˡ
of the Blue by
P.ᵉ Durell

Explanation of the Plan.		Explanation of the Prospect.		
A	Sallmadine Rocks	A	Strafford Adm.ˡ Vernon	G	Cumberland Fire Ship
B	Castle 23 Guns Moun.ᵗ	B	Princess Louisa	H	Terrible Bomb
C	Landing Place	C	Falmouth	I	Eleanor Fire Ship
D	Guard House	D	Norwich	K	Prize Brig
E	Draw Bridge	E	Alderney Bomb	L	Pompey Tender
F	Parade	F	Success Fire Ship	M	Goodly Tender
G	Trunk of a Tree			N	Prize Sloop
H	Log Wood Trees				It being Shots a good dist.ᵗ
I	Guard Coasts destroy'd				from Shore We were obliged
K	Custom House				to engage at a Mile distance
	Italick fig. depth in feet				Lat. of Chagre 9°. 20′. N.
	Roman fig. depth in fath.				Sold by William Herbert & Thomas Bowles
					in Cornhil & St Paul's Church Yard, London

A Prospect of the CASTLE and TOWN of CHAGRE

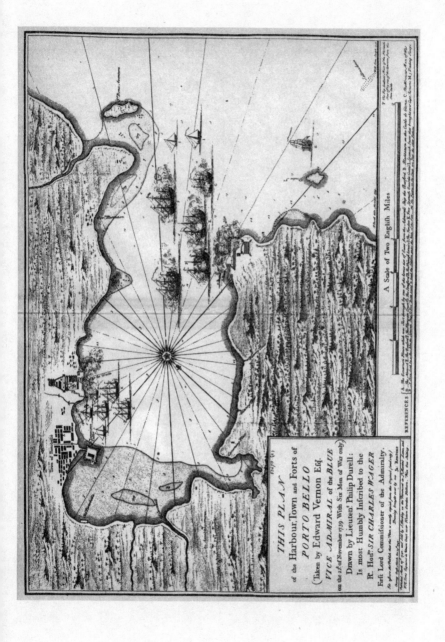

THIS PLAN
of the Harbour, Town and Forts of
PORTO BELLO
(Taken by Edward Vernon Esq.
VICE ADMIRAL of the BLUE
on the 2d of November 1739 With Six Men of War only)
Drawn by Lieutent Philip Durell:
Is most Humbly Inscribed to the
Rt Honble SIR CHARLES WAGER
First Lord Commissioner of the Admiralty.

A Scale of Two English Miles

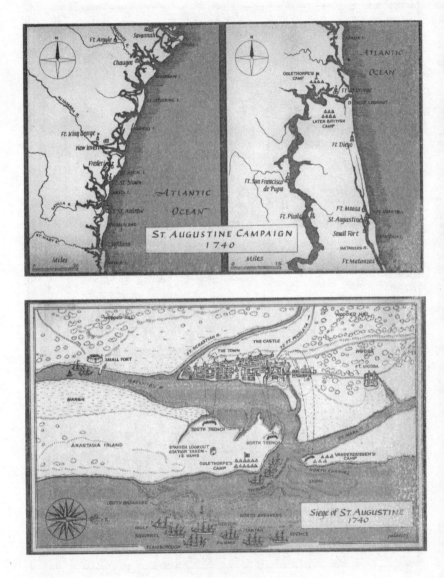

St. Augustine Campaign
1740

Siege of St. Augustine
1740

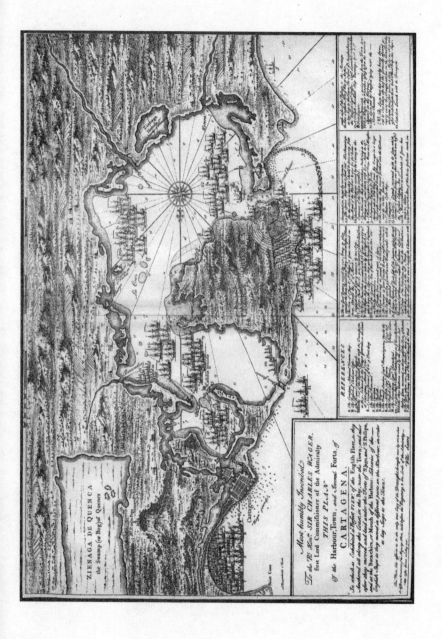

CONTENTS

At the Georgetown Flea

1.

The medal gleamed in the dealer's glass case. A tarnished disc, perhaps brass, about the size of an old half-dollar coin, resting incongruously beside pocket watches, silver cigarette cases, and an array of collectible spoons. Sun baked the asphalt; a hot wind blew from the direction of Wisconsin Avenue. A sweaty, heat-struck crowd shuffled between the booths. A few women carried sunbrellas; one man wore a sort of French Foreign Legion hat, the neck kerchief fluttering. This made a kind of sense; Washington, DC, in August is as hot as the Sahara, only with humidity.

The medal was crudely done, cartoonish even, and in dealer-speak had "some age on it," maybe a couple of hundred years.

The dealer, a large, shaggy man wearing a Hawaiian shirt stepped over, eager for a sale.

"That's a commemorative piece," he said. "British. Got some age on it."

"That's what I was thinking," I said. "But what does it commemorate?"

"Here—"

Without being asked, he opened the case, placed the medal on a velvet pad and handed me a magnifying glass.

The medal was encased in a clear plastic sleeve. It depicted an eighteenth-century gentleman, periwigged and wearing a tricorn hat, accepting a sword from a kneeling man dressed like a clown. In the kneeler's other hand a conical fez-like hat; above his head the words DON BLASS, with the "N" backward. Over his shoulder, a sailing ship that looked like it had been rendered by a child. Through the magnifying glass, I could just make out the inscription around the circumference, worn to a sheen by the years but not illegible: THE PRIDE OF SPAIN HUMBLED BY ADM. VERNON. The obverse showed the battlements of a fortified port city defended by cannon and watched over by a church with a tall spire. Four men-of-war stood at anchor in the wavy lines meant to indicate the waters of a bay beneath the city walls. Another inscription here read VERNON CONQUERED CATAGENA with the date APRIL 1 1741.

All this rang a very faint bell. I am a writer of historical narrative, but my era of specialization begins about a hundred years after the date on the medal and ends with the surrender of von Lettow-Vorbeck in the jungles of East Africa in 1919, the subject of my last book.

"What's your price on this?" I said at last.

"Six hundred," the dealer said. "It's a rare piece."

I dropped the medal to the velvet pad as if my fingers had just been burned.

"A little rich for my blood," I said.

"Look it up online," the dealer countered. "Search 'Admiral Vernon Medals,' check out the prices. Trust me, they're a thing."

I stepped away, but something stopped me. I hesitated. "Do you mind?" Then I pulled out my phone and snapped a few pictures of the medal, both front and back.

The dealer said he'd be here at the flea market in the same spot every Sunday for the rest of the month and that he had a little room to negotiate on the price. I'd do some research and get back to him, I said—but I didn't. I went to Nags Head to the beach the next weekend and the weekend after that it rained the tropical torrents we get here in late summer and the Georgetown Flea Market was reduced to a few sodden booths, their awnings dripping in the rain, and the dealer with the medal wasn't one of them.

2.

Months passed. I forgot about the odd little medal, about Admiral Vernon and the kneeling Don Blass. Then, one afternoon, going through the photos on my phone, deleting selfies and shots of the delicious pho at Rice Paper and the crab Benedict brunch at BlackSalt, I came across the photos of the medal and settled myself at my computer and searched "Admiral Vernon Medals" and sat back, astonished at what I found:

There wasn't just one Admiral Vernon medal but at least a thousand different varieties, so many that they constituted an entire subcategory in the field of numismatics. Scholarly tomes had been written on the subject going back to 1835, with Leander McCormick-Goodhart's authoritative study taking up a whole issue of *Stack's Numismatic Review* in 1945. McCormick-Goodhart, perhaps the most ambitious collector of these medals had amassed over ten thousand examples of nearly a thousand different types before his death in 1965. The most recent addition to what I suppose must be called "Admiral Vernon Medal Studies" came out less than a decade ago: *Medallic Portraits of Admiral Vernon*, cowritten by a pair of dedicated numismatists, John Adams and Fernando Chao, and published by Kolbe and Fanning Numismatic Books of Gahanna, Ohio. A first edition hardcover is available from Amazon for the exalted price of $149.85, shipping not included.

Meanwhile, several online coin auction sites featured a bountiful array of Admiral Vernon medals for sale, of several different kinds and qualities. Some of the medals were finely wrought, others looked like kindergarten blobs, but they all showed Vernon in various poses and in various places, some at Cartagena with the kneeling Don Blass, some at Chagres or Porto Bello—both located in present-day Panama. Several showed Vernon alone, looking stalwart, the pommel of his sword placed in such a way and at such an angle as to resemble a rather impressive erection. By far the most popular type depicted the Admiral standing in front of a town identified as PORTOBELLO WHICH HE TOOK WITH SIX SHIPS ONLY. A few of the rare ones showed Vernon as part of a triumvirate, like the famous statue of the Byzantine Tetrarchs built into the wall of the Basilica San Marco in Venice—Vernon's companions here identified as Ogle and Wentworth, whoever they were.

Medals depicting Vernon at Cartagena with the kneeling Don Blass—a few exactly like the one at the Georgetown Flea Market—were relatively plentiful, with examples ranging in price, depending on condition, from around $275 to $1,800. The Georgetown dealer's price of $600 seemed a little high for the condition of his medal, which looked like it might be rated somewhere between "F" for Fair and G for "Good" by the trade. In addition to the coin auction sites, the medals were available on eBay and Etsy—the latter offering them alongside beaded purses and hand-knitted kitty socks, used Doc Martens and other Etsy-friendly merchandise. The cheapest medal I found, on Seattle Craigslist, had lost the bottom third and most of the remaining details sometime during the last two hundred and seventy-odd years and could be purchased for a mere $29.

Suddenly, Admiral Vernon medals seemed as common as pennies in a penny jar. Could you find them down at the local Walmart? The sheer ubiquity of so many eighteenth-century medals honoring a British admiral I'd never heard of seemed to posit the existence of a parallel historical universe in which an outsized naval hero conquered his way through strange foreign cities where he was forever presented with the sword of a hapless harlequin named Don Blass. Were these real historical figures? Or the mythic figments of some long-gone medal-makers' imagination, a pot-metal British version of the Baron von Munchausen saga?

I decided to find out.

3.

Days in libraries turned into weeks, months, a year, and resulted in the modest volume you now hold in your hands. I learned many things during this period—among them that Admiral Vernon and the kneeling Don Blass did exist, along with Ogle and Wentworth, though not exactly as portrayed. "Don Blass" for example (a Spanish Basque Admiral, real name Blas de Lezo y Olavarrieta) never knelt to anyone, and not just because he had a wooden leg. And I learned that these four men and many others (including the great British novelist Tobias Smollett and a certain Captain Lawrence Washington, beloved half-brother of the better known George) were players in a forgotten conflict of vast proportions: a war in which an armada of transport vessels carried more than twenty-thousand British soldiers and sailors across the Atlantic to the West Indies to fight Spain as another squadron sailed around Cape Horn and into the Pacific all the way to the coast of China and on around the globe for the same purpose—arguably the first true "world war" known to history.

One of the most respected historians of the period, Harold W. V. Temperley, considers this forgotten war of such great import to subsequent events that the year it started, 1739, is to him "a turning point of history." Also, as Temperley says, the war prefigures modern conflicts as "perhaps, the first of English wars in which the trade interest absolutely predominated, in which war was waged solely for balance of trade rather than for balance of power."

Another historian, none other than the famous Thomas Carlyle, gave the war the funny name by which it is now generally known: the War of Jenkins' Ear. Though, for the record, he called it the War *for* Jenkins's Ear, a ridiculous moniker anyway, bequeathed to subsequent generations of historians and scholars offhandedly, in tiny type, in one of the many footnotes to his multivolume *History of Friedrich II of Prussia, Called Frederick the Great*, written more than a hundred years after the events in question. As Carlyle says:

> This War, which posterity scoffs at as the *War for Jenkins's Ear*, was, if we examine it, a quite indispensable one . . . a most necessary War, though of a most stupid appearance. A war into which King and Parliament, knowing better, had been forced by public rage, there being no other method left in the case.

Carlyle got his funny name for the war full of disease, disaster, and fatal miscalculation ("begun, carried on, ended as if by a people in a state of somnambulism!") from an infamous incident involving—yes—a severed ear, and a mariner named Jenkins, whom we'll meet in the ensuing pages. But the war itself, a contest between the British and Spanish empires in the Americas which lasted roughly four years and resulted in the deaths of thousands, wasn't funny at all.

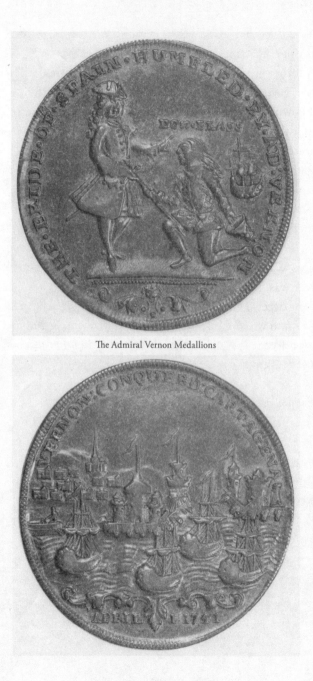

The Admiral Vernon Medallions

Sir Robert Walpole

ONE

The Incident

1.

On the morning of April 9, 1731, the British trading brig *Rebecca*, under the command of a tough, choleric Welshman by the name of Robert Jenkins, found herself becalmed in the dangerous waters off the Cuban coast, near Havana. She was London bound, out of Jamaica, carrying a load of sugar for the teas and cakes of England. From dawn, for hours, no wind stirred the *Rebecca*'s square-rigged sails; her spankers and booms hung slack in the hot, bright air as the sun rose.

April makes decent sailing weather in the Caribbean, hot and dry, comfortably removed from hurricane season, though occasionally afflicted with periods of deadly calm. The perilousness of the *Rebecca*'s situation in the Florida Straits that morning came not

1

from wind or wave or underwater obstruction, but from far more sinister man-made dangers: a long series of uncomfortable treaties between successive British monarchs (Queen Anne, George I and II) and Felipe V of Spain, fixing the spoils of war and the parameters of trade between the two countries.

These included the 1713 Treaty of Utrecht which brought the devastating War of Spanish Succession to an unsatisfactory conclusion; subsidiary treaties of December 14, 1715 and May 26, 1716, attempting to clarify certain vague clauses in the Treaty of Utrecht regarding British trading rights with Spanish colonies; the Treaty of London of 1718, establishing the Quadruple Alliance of Great Britain, France, the Holy Roman Empire, and the Dutch Republic against Spain; the Treaty of the Hague of February, 1720, which ended the misbegotten war resulting from that alliance; the Treaty of Madrid of June 1721 and the 1729 Treaty of Seville, officially ending the brief Anglo-Spanish War of the preceding two years.

All this diplomatic paperwork, engineered by royal negotiators in Madrid, London, and elsewhere had in the end created an impossible situation for Jenkins and his crew. According to "refinements" stipulated in the Treaty of Seville, any British merchant ship sailing near Spanish possessions in the West Indies might be stopped and searched for contraband trade goods or the proceeds from such, by the Spanish *guarda costa* (coast guard) at any time. Says historian Philip Woodfine:

> Once a ship had put in close to Spanish colonial coasts, it came under suspicion of being an illegal trader to settlements there, and became liable to investigation by the *guarda costas* who were commissioned to search and, where necessary, to seize vessels carrying contraband cargo. Ship and crew in such cases were conveyed to a nearby colonial port, where an enquiry, and often seizure, followed. It was enough

to have aboard the smallest quantity of Spanish Colonial produce, or the Spanish coin of 8 Reales, the "pieces of eight," which were the common currency of the whole Caribbean.

This much abused right of search-and-seizure had been negotiated and renegotiated between Spain and Great Britain as a part of the *Asiento de Negros*. This infamous contract, a monopoly granted by Spain to Britain in the Treaty of Utrecht, allowed the latter exclusive right to trade a fixed number of African slaves each year and a limited amount of manufactured goods to Spanish colonies in the Americas. On paper, the devil's bargain worked for both parties; in practice, the only way to turn a profit at *Asiento* trade was to turn smuggler.

The *guarda costa*'s fleet of fast, armed sloops had been commissioned by the Spanish government to interdict the smuggling everyone knew would inevitably arise—a mission that brought its own inevitable consequences. *Guarda costa* captains too often brutalized British crews and their captains and took whatever they wanted, including the ships in question, and occasionally the crews to use as convict labor, legal evidence of smuggling be damned. They generally acted, Temperley says, "as pirates toward the Englishmen, while posing as official vessels, very much the same way a clever thief robs a law-abiding citizen by impersonating a tax collector."

2.

Now, Captain Robert Jenkins watched with growing apprehension from the *Rebecca*'s taffrail as an oared sloop approached from the direction of the Cuban coast, a low green line about ten miles to the starboard. The vessel drew closer; Jenkins recognized it for a *guarda costa*, and his heart filled with dread. He had good reason for this uneasiness: scores of British ships had been taken in these waters, their cargoes ransacked and looted, their crews roughly handled, their captains tortured. Jenkins would have been generally familiar with the litany of recent outrages cited by merchant traders in England and later brought to the attention of the king in a series of increasingly aggrieved petitions. Here is a list of just a few of the claims:

The British galleys *Betty* and *Anne* seized, taken to Spanish ports and sold at auction, their crews imprisoned in filthy, vermin infested cells; the brig *Robert* taken, her captain, an Englishman named Storey King tortured for three days (*guarda costa* bravos had, among other cruelties, fixed lighted matches between Captain King's fingers and crushed his thumbs with gun-screws); the crew of the sloop *Runslet* taken, its crew abused with gun-screws in a similar manner, gun-screws apparently a popular form of torture on the Spanish Main that year; a captain named Thomas Weir, "maimed in both arms and confined to his berth" reportedly murdered by Spanish officials, along with eight of his men. And, most gruesomely, a Dutch captain's hand had been chopped off, the severed appendage boiled then fed to him one finger at a time. The Dutchman finished by eating the whole hand as *guarda costa* ruffians no doubt loomed about snickering, cutlasses drawn. One hesitates to imagine what he thought of this ghastly meal.

A few years later, in the anxious months leading up to war in 1739, King George II would send an irate memorandum to His Most Catholic Majesty, Felipe V of Spain, citing fifty-two British ships attacked and seized, with damages claimed in the hundreds of thousands of pounds—a mere fraction, British merchants asserted, of actual damages.

The most detailed account of what happened next to Captain Jenkins and the *Rebecca*, comes from an American source, Benjamin Franklin's *Pennsylvania Gazette* in the issue of October 7, 1731, six months after the incident. The wealth of detail offered by Franklin suggests he spoke to an eyewitness, perhaps one of the seamen aboard Jenkins's ship that fateful morning. A brief description of Jenkins's ordeal in the *Gentleman's Magazine* of June 1731, the captain's own deposition, and tidbits gleaned from correspondence between Thomas Pelham-Holles, the Duke of Newcastle, Secretary of State for the Southern Department and Benjamin Keene, British ambassador to the Spanish court, add descriptive flourishes—a bit of dialogue, a few conflicting details—to the dramatic scene Franklin presents.

3.

The *guarda costa* sloop, called either *La Isabela* or the *San Antonio*, depending on the source, drew closer across the glassy sea, her sixteen sweeps striking the water, rhythmic, inevitable. Presently, she came within hailing distance, but the sloop's captain eschewed the hailing-horn and began the conversation with three cannon shots across *Rebecca*'s bow. He then identified himself as Juan de León Fandiño, a notorious *guarda costa* privateer (or misidentified himself as the pseudonymous Juan Francisco, according to Franklin's account). Whatever his name and whatever the name of his ship (let's call him Fandiño of *La Isabela*, the generally accepted identity of both captain and vessel), he called for a delegation to bring the *Rebecca*'s sailing orders and cargo manifest to him for inspection.

Jenkins lowered the ship's boat and sent his first mate bearing only *Rebecca*'s clearances from the Governor of Jamaica, expecting "this document would give sufficient satisfaction, it being a Time of profound Peace with Spain." But Fandiño was not convinced by the clearances. He seized the hapless mate as a hostage and returned the boat bearing a dozen armed men. He then lowered his own boat and followed with another dozen. Once aboard, no courtesies were exchanged. Instead, Fandiño and his contingent of "swarthies," later described as "negroes, mulattoes, and Indians," set about ransacking the ship.

"They broke open all the Hatches, Lockers and Chests," looking for smuggled Spanish raw materials, generally "Logwood, Hides or Tallow, the Product of the Spanish settlements in America," or quantities of Spanish money generated from the illegal sale of British manufactured goods to Spanish colonists. Jenkins initially welcomed the search of his ship. He understood that per treaty agreement, the *guarda costa* as "the King of Spain's Officers . . . might do their duty, for there was nothing on board but which was the Growth and Produce of Jamaica," a chief British colony in the West Indies.

Fandiño's men spent the next two hours at their destructive task as Jenkins and his crew stood by helplessly. At last, finding nothing, Fandiño, in a rage, resorted to the terror tactics for which the *guarda costa* had become infamous in the West Indies. First, he lashed Jenkins to the foremast and forced the Welshman to watch as *guarda costa* ruffians brutally beat the *Rebecca*'s mulatto cabin boy in an effort to extract the location of any money hidden aboard. Perhaps it might be found in a secret compartment somewhere in the hold of the ship, as was often the case. But the cabin boy, knowing nothing, revealed nothing, and collapsed under the beating.

Though later commentators insist that Jenkins must have been a smuggler because everyone else was a smuggler in those days on the Spanish Main, no evidence has ever been found to support this claim. In fact, the known details of Jenkins's career supports the opposite conclusion: he seems to have been an honest merchant captain, trusted by his employers and bearing nothing more than a load of Jamaican sugar for the London exchange.

Fandiño, however, remained certain the *Rebecca* concealed hidden treasure; his efforts to find it grew increasingly frenzied. He tied the bleeding, insensate cabin boy around Jenkins's legs as dead weight, tightened a noose around the Welshman's neck and tossed the other end of the rope over a spar. Jenkins, unlashed from the mast, was then "hoisted up the Foreyard, but the boy, being light, slipt through . . . to the Captain's great ease." Fandiño ordered Jenkins hoisted into the yards two more times, each time "to the point of Strangulation." Each time he demanded Jenkins reveal the whereabouts of his treasure; each time the pugnacious Welshman asserted "that they might torture him to Death, but he could not make any other Answer."

Fandiño then threatened to burn the *Rebecca* to the waterline along with the crew, who as English Protestants were all "obstinate Hereticks," and thus good candidates for a Spanish Inquisition-style auto-da-fé. But even under threat of immolation, Jenkins still couldn't reveal the whereabouts of a treasure he didn't possess. Fandiño, mistaking innocence for stubbornness, left Jenkins gasping on the deck and conferred with his second-in-command, a man Franklin's account identifies as Lieutenant Dorce. Perhaps some fresh torture might be devised?

Dorce, "who had just put the rope around [Jenkins's] neck," then searched the Welshman's pocket, stealing a small amount of personal money he found there and also the silver buckles off Jenkins's shoes. At a gesture from Fandiño, his men then hung Jenkins again, this time leaving him dangling in the foreyards "until he was quite strangled." At the last possible moment, however, Fandiño ordered his men to release the rope. Jenkins dropped abruptly and with such force he bounced down the forward hatch, crashing onto the ship's casks of fresh water stored below.

From here, they dragged a bruised and bleeding but still alive Jenkins by the rope around his neck back up through the hatch. For a long time, he lay motionless on the hot deck, beside the broken form of his cabin boy. The long day waned. The sun, now high overhead, dropped in the west over the blue water and the distant coast of New Spain. How much longer could Fandiño and his men tarry aboard the *Rebecca*, dealing with these ridiculous Englishmen? Maybe there was no treasure aboard this ship after all. Fandiño decided to give it one last try. He ordered Jenkins bound to the mast again and taking up a cutlass and pistol charged at him screaming "Confess or die!"

But the unfortunate Jenkins could not confess. The ship's money included only what they had taken from his pockets and a small bag of coins—found in his cabin—reserved for operating expenses, consisting of "four Guineas, one Pistole and four Double Doubloons." A reasonable sum, but not enough to justify the seizure and ransacking of a British ship and the torture of its captain and crew. The *Gentleman's Magazine* picks up the narrative from here:

Fandiño, beside himself, "took hold of [Jenkins's] left ear and with his cutlass slit it down, and another of the Spaniards [Lieutenant Dorce?] took hold of it and tore it off, but gave him the Piece of his ear again and made threats against the King, saying 'the same will happen to him [King George II] if caught doing the same [i.e., smuggling].'" A statement rendered all the more absurd as Fandiño hadn't been able to find any smuggled merchandise aboard the *Rebecca*. (An image out of classical mythology suggests itself here: Jenkins bound to the mast like Odysseus approaching the rock of the Sirens—but head bowed, blood pouring down the side of his face, the most consequential severed ear in history lying on the bloody deck at his feet.)

Determined to commit a final barbaric act, Fandiño—according to Franklin's account—decided to scalp the much-insulted Jenkins; finding the Welshman's head too closely shaved, he gave up on this idea as impracticable. With daylight fading, and the general appetite for torture nearly sated, Fandiño's men contented themselves with beating the mate and boatswain "unmercifully." They then stripped the *Rebecca* of everything portable, including bedding and the clothes of the crew, leaving them standing naked on the deck. From Captain Jenkins they additionally took a "Watch of Gold, Cloathes, Linnens & etc. on a moderate valuation of 112 pounds, sterling." They also took a "tortoise shell box" and some old silverware.

Finally, Fandiño himself confiscated the *Rebecca*'s navigational equipment (maps, sextant, compass) and her store of candles— contraband, Fandiño asserted, made from Spanish tallow. More than an act of theft, a deadly act of sabotage designed to leave the *Rebecca* wallowing in darkness on unknown seas.

Later, in a letter of protest to the Spanish governor of Cuba, British Rear Admiral James Stewart, ranking naval officer at the Jamaica Station, cited the theft of the *Rebecca*'s navigational equipment as one of the most serious aspects of Fandiño's crime, as it indicated his intention had been "that she should perish in her passage [across the Atlantic]."

At last, Fandiño and his ruffians returned to *La Isabela* and sailed off. Jenkins' terrified and naked crew then quickly unbound their captain, brought him back to consciousness with rum and water and bandaged his bloody stump of ear. Immediately realizing the *Rebecca*'s predicament, a revived Jenkins set a course for the closest port, Havana, where he hoped to meet with another British ship from whom he "might procure sufficient necessities to enable him to proceed on his voyage"—and perhaps lodge an official complaint regarding the savage treatment he had received at the hands of the *guarda costas*. But Fandiño and *La Isabela* lurked just over the horizon. Coming alongside the British vessel once again, Fandiño called a warning to the mutilated Jenkins: make for open waters or this time he really would set the ship on fire!

So, "rather than have a second visit from them," Franklin reports, "captain and crew of the *Rebecca* recommended themselves to the Mercy of the Seas."

Crossing the Atlantic proved difficult. The crew made rudimentary garments out of sailcloth and sacking. Without candles, they burned oil and butter in the binnacle to steer by; without compass and sextant, Jenkins navigated by the stars and "by his nose," which is to say he used the excellent seamanship which would save his life and the lives of other crews time and again throughout his long career on the world's oceans. At last, after two months and "many Hardships and Perils," on June, 11, 1731, the *Rebecca* crossed the bar into the River Thames.

4.

Not long after Jenkins's return, his severed ear "preserved in a bottle," he personally presented an account of his suffering and the sufferings of his crew to King George II. Perhaps his Majesty might arrange for compensation for Jenkins's lost ear from the King of Spain. This audience, arranged by Secretary of State Newcastle at the behest of a group of London merchants, set off a brief diplomatic flurry. Furious letters flew back and forth between the Spanish and English courts; British Ambassador Benjamin Keene made a formal protest to the Spanish king; members of Parliament in opposition to the pacific policies of First Minister Robert Walpole agitated for a more vigorous attitude toward the Spaniards in the Caribbean. Rear Admiral Stewart again "specifically mentioned the case to the Spanish governor of Cuba as part of a series of complaints for which he demanded satisfaction."

Then, nothing happened.

The Jenkins matter was dropped and things went on as before. Anything, Walpole and his ministry believed, was preferable to war with Spain, which he guessed would be far more costly to commerce than a handful of ransacked ships and abused sailors. So the outrages of the *guarda costa* upon British trading vessels in the West Indies continued as British merchants—particularly the South Sea Company—hungry for profit, ramped-up their smuggling activities under the cover of the *Asiento de Negros*. Captain Robert Jenkins' ordeal, after "exciting some little attention" in the press of the day, all but faded from the national consciousness.

Years would pass before the British people heard of him again.

Emperor Charles II of Spain

TWO

Deep Background

FROM THE BEWITCHED KING TO THE SOUTH SEA BUBBLE,

1665–1720

1.

The War of Jenkins' Ear—or Carlyle's "War for Jenkins's Ear" or, to the Spanish, *la Guerra del Asiento*, or the "Anglo-Spanish War of 1739," so-called by modern historians, who like to suck the juice out of everything—perhaps became inevitable the day Felipe IV of Spain died. The Spanish king breathed his last on October 15, 1665, eyes fixed on the same miracle-working crucifix that had comforted his ancestors since the death of the great Holy Roman Emperor Charles V more than a hundred years earlier.

Though Felipe suffered from a variety of serious ailments—probably exacerbated by syphilis acquired from a lifetime's indulgence in the brothels of Madrid—it was thought at court that his demise had been the result of sorcery. In fact, evidence of a black magic assassination attempt had been uncovered: the bag supposed to contain holy relics always worn around the king's neck had been found to contain instead a miniature portrait of himself stuck with pins, a tiny book of evil spells, hair, teeth, and other Satanic odds and ends. The horrified priest who had discovered the contents of the bag quickly burned it on the altar of the chapel of Our Lady of Atocha—alas, too late. This exorcism could not save the king whose death had already been predicted by the appearance of a comet in the sky above Madrid in December 1664. Nor could it extinguish the darker fate brought on by generations of close inbreeding that now descended like a curtain on Spain's Hapsburg dynasty.

Dying, Felipe left his tragically deformed and perhaps imbecilic son, Carlos II, called *el Hechizado*, "the Bewitched," in possession of a globe-spanning empire. The new king's vast inheritance included half of Europe, the Spanish West Indies, the Philippines, Florida, that portion of South America not encompassed by Brazil, half of North America, and a few scattered cities on the North African coast. But along with all this excellent real estate came a nightmarish array of in-bred genetic infirmities. Carlos II's father and mother, for example, had been uncle and niece—a pattern repeated several times in preceding generations, going back to a schizophrenic ancestress named Joanna the Mad, every Hapsburg's crazy great-great-great-great grandmother. Carlos's degree of consanguinity, expressed by geneticists in the following terms: $F,(O.50)^3 \times(1)+(0.5)^3\times(1)=0.25$ added up to one of the highest possible inbreeding coefficients, an equation worthy of Satan himself.

Poor Carlos! Despite the presence of Spain's holiest relics at his birth (the three thorns from Christ's Crown of Thorns, a piece of the True Cross, a scrap of the Virgin Mary's mantle, the sacred walking stick of Santiago, and his miraculous belt) he failed to thrive. His sad eyes stare out at us accusingly across the centuries from dozens of royal portraits, though all the artifice of the court painters couldn't conceal the monstrosity they portray: His enormous misshapen head, terminating in the famous jutting "Hapsburg jaw," so misaligned that his teeth failed to meet, made it impossible to chew food (wet nurses fed him on breast milk through most of his childhood), while a huge tongue inhibited the ability to speak. His spindly legs barely supported the weight of his upper body. Thus unbalanced, Carlos was prone to falling, a tendency not improved by periodic epileptic fits.

When exhibited to the world in the first royal audience following the death of his father, Carlos at age six was unable to walk on his own. His nurses held him up by strings attached to his limbs, like a marionette.

"The King of Spain supported himself on his feet propped against the knees of his Menina who held him by the strings of his dress," wrote the French ambassador, M. de Bellefonds. "He covered his head with an English-style bonnet, which he had not the energy to raise. . . . He seems extremely weak, with pale cheeks and a very open mouth, a symptom, according to the unanimous opinion of his doctors, of some gastric upset . . . [they] do not fortell a long life, and this seems to be taken for granted in all calculations here."

Premature loss of teeth and hair, chronic dizziness, and suppurating ulcers—leaking what Carlos's doctors called "a laudable pus"—posit an additional diagnosis of syphilis inherited from his father. As does his frequent hallucinations and the long bouts of melancholy during which he held strange midnight conversations with the exhumed corpses of his royal predecessors. Ignorant of world affairs, barely able to read or write, his only playmates a surreal collection of dwarves, clowns, and continually lactating nurses,

Carlos had been deliberately undereducated by his powerful mother, Mariana of Austria, who sought to rule the kingdom on her own. Still, foreign ambassadors visiting the Spanish court found him lucid and reasonably intelligent, if under the thumb of his domineering mother and her favorites.

But Carlos's early death, constantly predicted, eagerly awaited by some, never came to pass. For thirty-five years after the puppet show of his first audience, he stubbornly refused to die. In his obstinacy, in his reverence for the Spanish Crown which he hoped to pass undiminished to another generation, and most of all in the enormity of his suffering, he might be accounted among the noblest of the Spanish Hapsburgs, second only to Charles V himself, Holy Roman Emperor and illustrious founder of the dynasty.

Unfortunately for Hapsburg dynastic survival, Carlos's most severe deficiency lay in the sexual realm. Married twice to women from aristocratic families of exemplary fertility, he failed to provide the required heir. Urologists now suspect that his habit of premature ejaculation had its causes in a "posterios hypospadias"—he passed urine and ejaculate through an opening half way down the penile shaft—or that he may have been intersex, with ambiguous genitalia.

2.

The greatest challenge of Carlos's fraught reign awaited him in his last weeks of life. Leaving no heir, he was forced to choose the next king of Spain, the inheritor of her European provinces and endless overseas empire. Two leading candidates emerged: a cousin, the Archduke Charles of the Austrian branch of the Hapsburgs, and Carlos's grandnephew, Philippe, Duc d'Anjou of the French House of Bourbon, grandson of Louis XIV, the glittering *Roi Soleil* of France.

Carlos wavered. Royal lawyers drew up two wills, the first favoring Archduke Charles, the second Philippe—which one would he sign? Europe held its breath. Most worried that Bourbon control of both France and Spain would ruin the carefully orchestrated balance of power that had kept Europe in a relative state of peace since the ruinous Thirty Years' War that had ended in 1648. Such a union, they said, would "level the Pyrenees," the spiky mountain range separating the two kingdoms, and create a massive superpower that might dominate the world.

Factions of the Spanish court and half of Europe lined up behind one candidate or the other: Austria, half of Spain (including Catalonia and Aragon), Portugal, the Dutch Republic, and certain German principalities of the Holy Roman Empire all backed the Archduke Charles. England (seven years before the Act of Union transformed her into Great Britain) also backed Archduke Charles. The rest of Spain, Louis XIV's France, Catholic Bavaria, and other ducal odds and ends backed Philippe.

On his deathbed, Carlos writhed in an agony of pain and indecision. His second wife, Maria Anna of Neuberg, nursed him tenderly through his final torments, feeding him "milk of pearls" (pearls crushed in wine or vinegar), standing by anxiously as the doctors put "cantharides" (the aphrodisiac Spanish Fly, which in a poultice does double duty as a blistering agent) on his feet, dead pigeons on his brow to cure his headaches, and laid the entrails of freshly slaughtered lambs on his stomach to keep him warm. Pulled this way and that, swayed by courtiers who favored the Archduke, now by those who favored the French candidate, Carlos finally stood on his own two feet, figuratively speaking: he signed the will naming Philippe d'Anjou as his heir—though, to become Felipe V of Spain, the latter would have to renounce any claims to the Crown of France.

Carlos fell back exhausted. He had just completed the hardest work of his life. He lingered in terrible pain for another week.

"Many people tell me," he gasped, "that I am bewitched, and I well believe it, such are the things I experience and suffer."

At last, on All Souls Day in 1700, he died, a "quintessence of weakness" but one upon which "men and women of strong will and fierce ambitions broke as against a granite rock."

The autopsy, performed by the court physician, probably exaggerates the extent of Carlos's deformities—but barely: "His corpse did not contain a single drop of blood," noted the autopsy report, "three large stones resided in his kidneys," also "his heart was the size of a peppercorn; his lungs corroded, his intestines rotten and gangrenous. He had a single testicle, black as coal, and his head was full of water." It is that solitary testicle, shriveled as a raisin, dangling over history like a curse, that in the end haunts the imagination.

The general opinion in Madrid, wrote the Austrian ambassador "is that the death is due to witchcraft."

3.

Whatever the cause of Carlos II's death, the last of the Spanish Hapsburgs had gone to meet the ancestors with whom he had so often conversed as they lay decomposing in their coffins. He had made his decision. But would the silver mines of Peru, the gold of the Incas, the orderly cities of the Spanish Netherlands, the rose-red castles of Aragon, the fat provinces of Italy, the galleons full of treasure, the numerous rivers and impenetrable forests of the New World, the plantations with their thousands of African and Indian slaves—would all of it go to a Frenchman without a fight because Carlos the Bewitched had scrawled his name on a bit of parchment?

A titanic struggle ensued over the resolution of this troubled bequest: the War of Spanish Succession. Its protracted sieges and bloody battles whose names, though fading, still echo down the centuries (Blenheim and Oudenarde, Ramilles and Denain and Malplaquet); its epic marches and countermarches and grand strategies; the famous soldiers on both sides, the incomparable John Churchill, Duke of Marlborough, great-great-great-grandfather of Winston; the brave, diminutive Prince Eugene of Savoy; the magnificent French Marshals, Villars and Vendome and Bouffleurs—all this is best reserved for another volume.

Suffice to say that at Malplaquet, on September 11, 1709, over a period of seven hours 30,000 men died. It was the bloodiest battle of the eighteenth century—indeed, one of the bloodiest in history to that point—with a single-day butcher's bill unequaled until World War I's Maxim guns and gas attacks. British soldiers fighting over the same ground in 1914 reportedly discovered skeletons lying beside rusted muskets in sunken earthworks crossing the Wood of Sars, scraps of red cloth stuck to the bones, all from the 1709 clash. (The battlefield in Northern France remains remarkably unchanged today—the same bleak fields, the same woods and thickets. There are one or two crumbling monuments; grass has grown over the graves of the dead. In the nearby village of Taisnieres, in a café on the *place*, you can drink a *Cognac fine a l'eau* not far from the spot where the cavalry of the *Maison du Roi*, led by Boufflers himself, charging six times, drove Prince Eugene's Allied cavalry back through the battered redoubts.)

The slaughter at Malplaquet sickened a Europe poised on the threshold of the Age of Enlightenment, but it did not end the war. Shortly after the battle, Britain rejected a peace treaty offered by Louis XIV granting all the Allies major demands. The French king even acceded to Charles of Austria's elevation to the Spanish throne—cutting out his own grandson—against the advice of Marshal Villars, who saw the Allied victory over the French at Malplaquet as pyrrhic. "The enemy cannot afford many such victories," he told his royal master. But Marlborough wanted to crush

France. Nothing less than the total destruction of Louis's showy regime would answer his ambitions.

The blood of Malplaquet soaked slowly into the ground.

4.

Six years later, with the great Marlborough deposed and discredited by his political enemies, England at last made a separate peace with France and Spain. She thus broke a promise to her allies to fight on; the Dutch in disgust closed the gates of their fortresses to retreating, exhausted English troops who had thrown down their arms.

The terms of the peace looked like this: Charles of Austria formally renounced his claims to the Spanish throne; Spain retained her overseas empire but relinquished her provinces in Northern Europe, including the Spanish Netherlands (present day Belgium), Luxembourg, and her provinces in Italy (Milan, Naples, Sicily), but kept her French Bourbon king who renounced his right to inherit the French throne. Gibraltar and Menorca went to England; Sicily to Savoy; Sardinia to Austria. European maps had to be redrawn; territory and allegiances shifted. As Carlos the Bewitched had intended, Philippe, Duc d'Anjou would now be acknowledged by all as His Most Catholic Majesty Felipe V of Spain. He began a long, weird reign during which he would exhibit his own share of Hapsburg madness, inherited through the maternal line.

And yet, England's armies under Marlborough had been largely victorious. She would be compensated for her success on the battle-field. She was now in a good position to acquire through negotiation long-sought trading rights with Spain's South American colonies as one of the spoils of war. These trading rights embodied in the noto-rious *Asiento de Negros*—the exclusive contract to supply African slaves to Spain's South American colonies—had been held by France for the previous dozen years.

5.

The history of the *Asiento de Negros* begins in 1517 when Holy Roman Emperor Charles V (also Carlos I, King of Spain) granted the original slaving contract to a court favorite, a Flemish nobleman, Laurent de Gouvenot. Not wishing to sully his hands with commerce of any kind, particularly not with the dirty business of slaving, Gouvenot immediately sold his contract to a cabal of Genoese merchants based in Seville for 25,000 ducats.

The Portuguese had dominated the nascent trade in African slaves for the hundred years or so preceding the first *Asiento*. Bartolomeu Dias, the Portuguese mariner, rounded the Cape of Good Hope in 1418, the first European to do so. Where he went, Portuguese slavers would follow. African slaves worked sugar plantations on the Portuguese island of Madeira as early as 1460; the Portuguese built the first European slave fort off the coast of what is now Ghana in 1481. Most have forgotten that the Portuguese were the original European explorers of West Africa, the original European colonizers, the original European slave traders.

In the early years of Spain's empire in the New World, colonists made use of an easily accessible labor source—the indigenous inhabitants of the Americas—whose abuse the Dominican Friar Bartolomé de las Casas decried in his famous, controversial tract *A Brief Account of the Destruction of the Indies*. After twenty-five years of harsh Spanish rule, a brief generation, the indigenous population of New Spain had nearly collapsed. Wars, torture, insurrection, but mostly disease, had swept away untold thousands. Ravished from pristine forests by brutal conquerors, uprooted from a state of primeval freedom, the native people preferred to die rather than work the silver mines and bean fields for their Spanish oppressors. Thus, the importation of enslaved Africans became necessary for the survival of Spain's colonial enterprise.

But few Spaniards cared to pursue the lamentable trade. Nor were the resources available in Spain (the ships and men, the expert knowledge of African coasts) so they farmed it out to others via the *Asiento*. The original 1517 contract offered a monopoly of the slave trade for eight years, with a maximum of 4,800 slaves sold per year to Spain's colonies, divided between male and female, young and old for a price not exceeding 45 ducats per slave. An additional complication divided each slave into fractions of a slave called *piezas de Indias*—literally "Indian Pieces"—units of trade that graded each slave like a slab of supermarket beef graded today by the USDA.

"When a slave ship arrived in a Spanish-American port, the royal officers examined the negroes for disease and measured them as so many units of *piezas de Indias* in order to compute the duties due to the King of Spain," writes John G. Sperling, one of the foremost experts on the *Asiento*. "Negroes in perfect health were counted as follows: from 5 to 10 years they equaled ½ of a *pieza*, from 10 to 15 they equaled ⅔, from 15 to 30 they equaled 1, and above thirty they equaled ¾. Smallness, deformity or sickness altered the measurements."

(This idea—that a single enslaved African might be divided into fractions of himself—had a discomfiting afterlife. Surely its echo can be seen in the Three-Fifths Compromise at the US Constitutional Convention of 1787, in which delegates agreed, for the purposes of census taking, to count slaves as ⅗ of a human being.)

From Gouvenant and the Genoese, the *Asiento de Negros* quickly passed back to the Portuguese and through many other hands, though, like a hot potato, none held it very long: A succession of Portuguese merchants through the sixteenth century gave way to the Dutch in the seventeenth. Despite their blindingly white lace and Calvinistic probity, the Dutch made enthusiastic slavers. In the end, sharp business practices and Dutch-Spanish hostilities brought them down. Then, in 1702, the French, in the guise of a state-owned enterprise called *la Compagnie de Guinée*, received the *Asiento* as a reward for backing their own candidate, the Archduke Charles, for the Spanish throne in 1700.

It had taken the War of Spanish Succession to reverse this bequest.

6.

In Bristol they called him the "Sunday Gentleman." A failed hosiery salesman, cat farmer, tile maker, importer of Spanish wines—also an inexhaustible pamphleteer, political journalist, novelist, and all-around literary genius—named Daniel Defoe. But geniuses generally make terrible businessmen. In those days, debt was a criminal offense; debtors' prison loomed for the insolvent. Often on the run from the collapse of one-or-another moneymaking scheme, some plausible, some ridiculous, Defoe fled London for Bristol in March 1692. (All this happened about fifteen years before he sat down to write a book called *Robinson Crusoe*. Only the Bible has been translated into more languages.)

In Bristol, Defoe hid from the authorities, firing off letters to London friends begging loans; to creditors, craving indulgence; to his disappointed wife, explaining himself: Admittedly, the cat-farming hadn't gone well. These weren't ordinary cats, but civets, valued for scent glands indispensable to the making of strong perfumes in a stinky age. Picture cages full of angry felines awaiting their fate at the hands of the gland extractors and the difficulties of such an undertaking becomes clear. Also, he had sold the cats to two different investors simultaneously while defrauding his mother-in-law of 400 pounds. Even after the lapse of three centuries, you can almost hear the writer equivocating: he'd had no choice, he was very sorry, but he needed the money and had to unload the cats.

Like most writers, Defoe had a taste for showy clothes: lace cuffs, velvet coats, silver-buckled shoes; not to mention the extravagant wigs of the era, rising above his steep forehead like a cumulonimbus full of heat lightning. He emerged from his secret Bristol lair every Sunday in his best duds to stroll the town since custom forbade the arrest of debtors on Sundays—hence the "Sunday Gentleman."

A decade and many schemes later, authorities caught up with the dandyish Defoe at last. Government wanted posters offering fifty pounds for information leading to his arrest described him as

> the author of slanderous and seditious Publications . . . a middle-sized, spare man, about 40 years old, of a brown Complexion . . . wears a Wig, a hooked Nose, a sharp chin, grey Eyes, and a large mould near his Mouth. Was born in London and was for many years a hose factor . . . a Seditious man of a disordered mind and a person of bad name, reputation and Conversation.

An acquaintance betrayed him to the authorities; since the days of Judas there's always been some rat around willing to perform this function for cash. Convicted of "Seditious Libel," the writer received a heavy sentence at the hands of a notorious hanging judge with the sinister name of Salathiel Lovell: first, three days in the pillory at Stoke-Newington, a stone's throw from the Defoe family home (this location deliberately chosen for its humiliation value), then a heavy fine and incarceration in the dreadful Newgate Prison until that fine might be paid in full. For a man of Defoe's epic insolvency, this amounted to a life sentence. And yet he feared the pillory most of all. Men had died on the pillory, head and hands locked in the iron stocks, pissing themselves, exposed to the weather and the abuse of sadistic crowds, pelted with rotten vegetables, stones, excrement.

Defoe, tougher than he looked, survived the pillory, and was eventually freed from Newgate's "stench and nastiness" by a political enemy, a prominent Tory politician, Robert Harley, later Earl of Oxford. Let's consider for a moment the political landscape in England of Defoe's day. English parliamentary politics of the eighteenth century allowed for only two parties, Tory and Whig. The former generally aristocratic, conservative, isolationist, on the side of a strong monarchy; the latter generally middle-class, business oriented, and comparatively progressive, in favor of more liberty for more people as long as those liberties coincided with the making of money. The nation swayed back and forth between these two poles. The Whig vs. Tory political struggle—marked by assassination attempts, power grabs, and deadly rivalries—at times played out like a Jacobean revenge play, but no more corrosive to the public good than the bitter party politics of our own era.

Even by eighteenth-century standards, Robert Harley was an alcoholic. Heavy drinking affected his behavior and speech; he was often drunkenly inarticulate in the presence of the reigning monarch, Queen Anne. When Harley did manage to get the words out, it was not easy to understand what he meant, complained the poet Alexander Pope.

"That lord," Pope asserted, "spoke with serpentine convulsions and talked of business in so confused a manner that you did not know what he was all about; and everything was in the epic way, for he always began in the middle." Harley "flustered himself daily with claret," added the historian Macauley, though this drinking habit, "was hardly considered a fault by his contemporaries." It was a hard-drinking age.

Claret-flustered or not, Harley possessed a clear political vision. He knew England would most probably soon acquire the *Asiento de Negros* from Spain as spoils of war, and that the nation would have to create a vehicle to administer this acquisition. And he needed Defoe's genius to help him devise a scheme that would harness the *Asiento*'s potential for profit-making and enrich both himself and the nation in the process. The writer had long been fascinated by the South American continent—specifically that part bordering the "South Seas," by which he meant Chile's lengthy Pacific coast and the coast of Peru, an area that would later become the fictional setting for his masterpiece *Robinson Crusoe*. Defoe thought the "South Sea Coast" of South America ripe for exploitation, the perfect arena for British investment and colonization. As Defoe wrote in *An Essay on the South-Sea Trade* in 1709:

> Great Quantities of Silver which the French squadrons, and Private Merchant Ships, have brought Home from the South-Seas have been spoken of . . . frequently accompanied with Reflections, and a general Regret, that these happy Advantages should pass by us. That the English nation, who are so much better qualified in every Way, both by their Manufactures to Trade with, Islands to Trade From, and Naval Strength to manage and protect that Trade, should so long lie still and leave unattempted a Trade, which in the Enemies Hand, is so fatal to us, and which in our Hands might be so fatal to them.

He further recommended "the Planting of our own People in those Rich Climates, where, by laying a Foundation of Trade which was never yet ingaged in, Our Subjects might come to be enrich'd."

And so on for several thousand words.

England's acquisition of the *Asiento* would dovetail nicely with Defoe's South American fantasies and Robert Harley's political schemes.

Meanwhile, created Chancellor of the Exchequer in 1710, Harley faced an insurmountable national debt brought on by the War of Spanish Succession, nearing its tenth year. The nation's "floating," that is, short-term debt, largely caused by the war, now stood at nearly ten million pounds and threatened economic stability.

"This 'unfunded' debt in the form of tallies, interest arrears, and other claims on government spending" explains forensic economist and historian Richard Dale, "would be rolled over if it could not be refinanced longer term. By 1711, interest arrears had built up and . . . was being traded in the secondary market at deep discounts averaging around 32%." National insolvency, a black mountain covered with ice, grew ever higher, looming over everyone's shoulder.

Harley wanted a single scheme to solve several key matters, all intertwined; one that might: (1) lessen the government's dangerous level of indebtedness, (2) secure a profitable peace with France and Spain, and (3) reduce the financial power of Harley's Whig political enemies.

For inspiration, he turned to his creature, Defoe. The writer soon dreamed up a concept of characteristic genius, eventually known as the "South Sea Scheme," which Harley just as characteristically presented as entirely his own—despite Defoe's contributions and the involvement of a trio of shady "stock jobbers" (speculators), Elias Tuner, Jacob Sawbridge, and George Caswall.

These men hoped for immense profits from the Defoe/Harley scheme which advocated the creation by act of Parliament of a public-private joint-stock corporation to be called the "South Sea Company." This company would eventually derive—it was assumed—vast profits from the *Asiento* trade. It would also privatize the vast national debt by "persuading [the government's] creditors to accept shares in the South Sea Company as payment. The Government would be relieved of an enormous burden . . . and would only need to find the money to pay the interest."

7.

On September 8, 1711, after a season of heavy politicking and a couple of assassination attempts against his life, Harley at last pushed the South Sea Company through Parliament, with himself as its first governor. This trading firm, derisively dubbed "Harley's Masterpiece" by the skeptical Whig opposition, would become the commercial vehicle to administer the *Asiento*, should it land in England's lap—which everyone counted on. From the beginning, the South Sea Company took shape as an unholy public-private partnership, ripe for exploitation by unscrupulous politicians and financiers, with shares traded in the coffee houses of "Exchange Alley," London's eighteenth-century version of Wall Street.

A corrupt speculator named John Blunt drafted the company charter, taking the Bank of England as a model. Blunt however added certain stipulations that made stock manipulation and corruption inevitable. Following Harley's tenure as governor, "control of the Company would pass to a small group of directors," explains Sperling—a fraction of the Company's unwieldy thirty-three member board, who would be "given the unique power to act in anything committed to them as fully as the entire Court of Directors might lawfully do. This seemingly innocuous provision was designed . . . to enable them to take over power once the politicians had left the scene."

The governorship eventually became a figurehead position and later passed to the ruling monarch, King George I. Any criticism of the Company's financial dealings thus became tantamount to treason.

The South Sea Company quickly established its headquarters in an impressive new building at the corner of Threadneedle Street and Bishopsgate in London. It was granted a coat of arms by the College of Heralds, described in heraldry speak as "Azure, a globe wheron are represented the Straits of Magellan and Cape Horn all proper and in sinister chief point two herrings haurient in saltire argent crowned or, in a canton the united arms of Great Britain." Translation: two crossed fishes wearing crowns dangling over a map of the ass end of the world. They took as their motto "From Cádiz to the Dawn," a reference to the Spanish port city of Cádiz, from which Spain's treasure galleons traditionally set out for the West Indies.

To go along with this fanciful logo, the South Sea Act granted the Company an equally fanciful monopoly on trade with "the kingdoms, lands etc of America, on the east side from the river Aranoca [Orinocco], to the most southern part of the Terra del Fuego, on the west side therof, from the said most southern part through the South Seas to the most northern part of America, and into, unto and from all countries in the same limits reputed to belong to the Crown of Spain, or which shall be hereafter discovered." Additionally, the Company would receive "an annual payment from the Exchequer of £568,279, to be secured on specific customs revenues . . . representing 6 percent return on £9.5 million of outstanding short-term government debt." This to be converted by its holders into South Sea Company stock:

> "The Company would acquire claims to the same value against the government," in what Richard Dale calls "a large-scale debt-equity swap. . . . In less than ten years the South Sea Company was to become a corporate monster with a market capitalization of over £200 million, although like the modern dot.com equivalent, its trading operations remained minimal and mostly loss-making."

Two years later, the South Sea Company, to this point something of an empty vessel, received the bitter liquor for which it had been designed: according to the Treaty of Madrid, signed on

March 26, 1713, as part of the general Utrecht agreement, Great Britain at last officially became the twenty-fifth recipient of the *Asiento de Negros* slave trading contract in just under two hundred years. It was a dream of cornucopia, an inexhaustible source of gold bullion, silver ingots, and emeralds in exchange for African slaves and British manufactured goods. But this dream came with responsibilities. The contract to be administered by the South Sea Company, boiled down, looked like this:

1. English "Asientists" were required to transport the traditional 4,800 *piezas de Indias* annually to Spanish America each year for thirty years—a *pieza* being here defined as an African slave between the ages of fifteen and thirty, at least fifty-eight inches tall, with no physical defects.
2. Payment for both African slaves and trade goods could be received in money, gold, silver bullion, or "fruits of the country," that is, via barter.
3. African slaves could be carried by English vessels to all Spanish-American ports.
4. English Asientists had the right to send each year a single *navio de permiso*—permission ship—containing 500 tons of trade goods to the fairs at Cartagena, Porto Bello, or Vera Cruz. The King of Spain was to receive 28¾ percent of the profits from this venture.
5. Factories, comprising warehouses, slave pens, offices, and living quarters, staffed by four to six Englishmen could be established to carry out the *Asiento* trade, but they could not be fortified.

Sperling concludes:

This contract was drawn up on the assumption that Spain's colonial system accorded with Spanish colonial theory, and that the *Asiento* company would adhere to the terms of the agreement. "Unfortunately, the agreement was incapable of working smoothly. No amount of explanation or clarification of the terms of the contract, nor bribing of Spanish officials could mask the incompatibility between the Company and the Spanish colonial system.

By the end of 1713, the Company was ready to engage in the new transatlantic "negro trade" to the Spanish colonies. They had set up factories in Porto Bello, Cartagena, Vera Cruz, Havana, Caracas, and Buenos Aires and transported 1,540 African slaves before the fall of 1714.

More slave ships followed; most of their human cargo was purchased from British Royal African Company's castles along the Guinea Coast, and from private traders at the slave "refreshment stations" at Jamaica or Barbados. But the Spanish objected to slaves who had spent more than a few days in English colonies, regarding them as possibly "tainted with Protestantism," and dangerous to the Catholic faith. What they wanted were *bozales*, slaves brought directly from Africa—and thus generally considered adherents of a primitive animism and ripe for conversion. For their part, Jamaican slave dealers regarded the latter as potentially diseased (infected with yellow fever, malaria, and other tropical maladies) and imposed an illegal tax on each slave, over and above the duties already required by both the Spanish and British crown.

"The many disabilities under which the slave trade labored inclined the South Sea directors to consider various plans—to contract with other traders to supply the negroes, or to allow trade by license," Sperling explains. "This would lead one fairly naturally to the conclusion that *the slave trade was not profitable* . . . the tendency of the Spanish officials to reduce their value by registering them as *pieza de India* rather than by head, loss of negroes through sickness and finally the competition from interlopers made it a losing game."

Here we are confronted with one of the great ironies of a history, already replete with too many: That the "legal" slave trade, though possessed of a certain dark glamour, was not profitable. And the annual permission ship couldn't legally carry enough trade cargo to cover the loss. Still, the South Sea Company tried to make it work. Four trade ships sent between 1714 and 1718 netted the Company £105,250—no great amount for a trading concern that had been founded on vast golden dreams, but roughly 75 percent of legal profits made over a twenty-five-year period. This left only the "illegal" smuggling of British manufactured goods in slave ships as a reliable source of profit.

Thus, the shadow of corruption falls early across the already shadowy business of the South Sea Company. No doubt the entire system of Anglo-Spanish trade as organized under the *Asiento* would have been renegotiated, more in England's favor—as South Sea grumblers soon demanded. But another Anglo-Spanish war ended both legal and illegal commerce abruptly with a few well-placed cannon shots off Cape Passaro, Sicily, in August 1718.

8.

We now return to Spain, groaning beneath the haphazard administration of her first Bourbon king, Felipe V. Hagridden, melancholic, prone to fits of antic madness alternating with episodes of catatonic lethargy, he had inherited more than his share of Hapsburg afflictions—a worthy successor to his "bewitched" great-uncle, Carlos II. And, like Carlos, he was tenacious: for forty-six years, longer than any other Spanish monarch, Felipe held the throne like a captain clinging to the bridge of a sinking ship.

The Hapsburgs and their cousins, the Bourbons, alternated from one generation to the next between extreme libidinousness—Felipe IV, Carlos's father, had produced at least thirty known bastards—and a kind of sex-phobia, symbolized by Carlos II's uncertain genitalia. Felipe V seemed to combine both impulses in one person: though a devout and morbidly superstitious Catholic, horrified by the thought of adultery, his carnal appetites rose to the level of a sex addiction—which could only be slaked in the flesh of his wife. Married at seventeen to the thirteen-year-old Maria Luisa of Savoy, Felipe became, as one biographer put it, "a passionate slave to lovemaking." Exhausted by her husband's constant physical demands, Maria Luisa produced four children before succumbing to tuberculosis a few years later.

Felipe, "persuaded only with difficulty to forsake his wife's bed the night before she died," acted with apparent indifference afterward, eschewing her funeral for the usual day's hunting. He watched from a distance, astride his horse, as Maria Luisa's cata-falque wound its way toward the Escorial Palace, that gloomy pile wherein lies entombed Spain's royal dead. Then he wheeled about without a word and hoofed it back into the woods. Of course, no one can say what grief filled his secret heart that day. But the great eighteenth-century French diarist Saint-Simon reacted with his usual acerbity when told of this incident:

"Princes, are they human?" he asked.

Perhaps not.

Denied the pleasures of the marriage bed by the early death of his wife, and refusing to accept the consolations of a mistress, Felipe suffered from cold sweats, headaches, and nightmares every bit as terrifying as those which had afflicted Carlos II. Soon, he fell into a fit of melancholy and refused to get up in the morning. Clearly, a suitable bride had to be found before the king's sexless condition drove him completely mad. Several candidates emerged and were rejected: a Bavarian princess—too ugly; a Portuguese princess—a known harridan; another Savoyarde—too capricious; a French duchess—too French. (The mood in the Spanish court, forever flip-flopping, had recently turned against France, Spain's erstwhile ally.)

An acceptable candidate finally emerged: twenty-two-year-old Elizabeth Farnese, Princess of Parma. This small but strategic principality, then as now known for its pungent cheeses and other culinary delicacies, lay sandwiched between Tuscany and the Papal States. Elizabeth, the step-daughter and niece of the current duke (her mother had married her deceased husband's brother) had been proposed by Parma's ambassador to Spain, a talented and completely unscrupulous priest-diplomat named Giulio Alberoni. Some said Alberoni suggested this match sotto voce at Maria Luisa's funeral; most considered him too wily for such an ill-timed breach of etiquette—though they otherwise described him as an unprincipled adventurer who would stop at nothing to advance Parma's interests, as long as those interests coincided with his own.

Born in the tiny village of Fiorenzuola d'Arda, the son of an impoverished gardener and a seamstress, as a youth Alberoni had earned a few pennies ringing the bells at the Duomo in Piacanza, the nearest large town. There, he'd been singled out for his vivid personality and precocious intelligence by the pastor and educated at parish expense. Entering Parma's diplomatic corps, he quickly rose in the service of his country. Saint-Simon, fond of scandalous tales, relates the following anecdote: During the War of Spanish Succession, the Duke of Parma sent Alberoni as special envoy to the notoriously rude French soldier, the Duc de Vendome. Alberoni resisted outrage when Vendome, in a typical display of contempt for all priests, defecated and wiped his ass in Alberoni's presence. Alberoni's predecessor, the Bishop of Parma had previously stalked out at this crude, oft-repeated display, resigning his position in a huff. The adroit Alberoni instead knelt and kissed the Duc's poopy posterior, exclaiming *"O culo di angelo!"* This quite literal brownnosing amused the Duc and made Alberoni's name in European diplomatic circles.

Before long, the ex-bellringer found himself hobnobbing with field marshals and kings as Parma's ambassador to Spain. His rapid rise can't be accounted for by natural intelligence alone, or a nicely timed talent for flattery. Alberoni was also an excellent chef, famous for his complicated and delicious pasta dishes. Now he made good use of what has been called his "sausage and pasta diplomacy"— mated with a low-down, Mafiaesque cunning—to seduce allies and enemies alike into supporting the Parmegian candidate for the Queen of Spain. Alberoni's "voluminous correspondence . . . is an incredible catalogue of detailed orders for hams, cheeses, olives and truffles," one biographer wrote. "Delays, or the shipment of less than choice items, brought reproaches that carefully planned friendships at court were at stake."

The statesman-priest-chef Alberoni learned an important lesson in his years as Parma's ambassador: that a well-prepared *Coppa del Cardinale*—the savory pork dish named after him—served with a side of *Agnolini Parma*, a nice green salad, and a decent Lambrusco could work diplomatic miracles.

9.

On September 16, 1714, Felipe V and Elizabeth Farnese, Princess of Parma—henceforth known as Isabela, Queen Consort of Spain—wed by proxy in Parma's cathedral. On Christmas Day, after a refresher ceremony performed by the Patriarch of the Indies, Felipe and his new queen consummated their union in the village of Guadalajara, Spain. In those days, Spanish royal weddings were often celebrated in such out-of-the-way impoverished hamlets, as tradition exempted residents from taxation for a year: marriage in a large city might have bankrupted the state treasury.

Felipe emerged from the bridal chamber the next morning, wobble-legged and satiated, delighted with his lusty, young Italian wife. It was more than love this time, he told a courtier, he was now her "slave for life." Indeed, Isabela soon established herself as the dominant power in Spain. Though she later ran to fat and walked with a limp, one imagines her, in this period as lush and infinitely desirable—looking a little like the earthy Italian actress Claudia Cardinale at twenty-four years old, in Visconti's classic film *Il gattopardo*—that masterful, melancholy evocation of an aristocracy in decline. Initial reports, engineered by Alberoni, had falsely described her as demure and biddable; the opposite was in fact the case: strong-willed and acid-tongued, Isabela soon earned the sobriquet bestowed by British diplomats at Madrid. To them, she was the "Spanish Termagant."

There had been earlier warnings of Isabela's strident personality. She had refused to accept Felipe's marriage proposal until covered with the jewels of her choice—among these a heart shaped necklace composed of 130 perfect pearls, a rosary of massive coral beads and an emerald ring weighing 74 carats. The Spanish "Plate Fleet" of 1715, already loaded down with three years' worth of silver and gold, lingered at Havana weeks into hurricane season, waiting for Isabela's jewels to arrive from far-flung corners of the empire. On July 31, a murderous storm caught them outward bound in the Florida Straits. Scattered by hundred-mile-per hour winds, eleven of the twelve heavily laden galleons foundered on reefs or capsized; 1500 sailors perished.

Two hundred and fifty years later, legendary treasure hunter Kip Wagner located the first wreck site off what is now Vero Beach, Florida—perhaps the *Nuestra Señora de Nieves*, Our Lady of the

Snows. Eventually, he dredged up millions in silver cobs and gold ingots. The Queen's jewels, however, are still buried somewhere in the reefy shallows off Florida's "Treasure Coast."

10.

The weak-willed, sex-addicted Felipe soon relinquished the running of the kingdom to his wife, retiring to bed for increasingly long stretches. His Hapsburgian tendency toward depression gradually metamorphosed into a kind of hysterical anxiety; this now alternated with the catatonia he'd already displayed. He came to rely on Isabela in all matters and couldn't be away from her for more than thirty minutes without suffering a nervous collapse. He moved into the Queen's apartments where both slept in the same bed—an outlandish habit that scandalized the court.

"[Felipe] loves his wife above all things, leaves all affairs to her and never interferes with anything," commented a contemporary observer. "He is very pious and believes he should be damned if he committed any matrimonial infidelity. But for his devotion, he would be a libertine, for he is addicted to women, and for this reason he is so fond of his wife . . . and because he is very easily led, the Queen won't lose sight of him."

The ubiquitous Saint-Simon, on a visit to Spain, writes of being received by the king and queen "in a bed of four and a half feet at most, of crimson damask with four bed posts." The king, dressed in a sleeping cap and his wife's dirty nightgown, lay propped on pillows beside her while she embroidered. State papers lay scattered about, the Queen's yarn balled atop trade agreements and diplomatic correspondence.

Physical charms aside, Isabela came encumbered with a heavy piece of political baggage—carried on her behalf by Alberoni: the recovery of those Spanish territories in Italy stripped and handed off to Austria and Savoy by the Treaty of Utrecht. The children of Felipe's first marriage to Maria Luisa would rule Spain by hereditary right, with Isabela's own children—eventually six in number—reduced to secondary roles. For them, the Spanish throne itself would be forever out of reach.

Isabela's ambitious nature found this certainty unacceptable. Her own father, Odoardo, Duke of Parma and her father/uncle, Francesco, also Duke of Parma, had died with no legitimate offspring; her second uncle the current Duke also seemed unlikely to reproduce before his demise. This would naturally leave her first son Carlos, Infante of Spain as the inheritor of the Duchy. Seized with a kind of desperation, she became obsessed with the idea of obtaining an Italian kingdom for her second son. Urged on by Alberoni, she schemed to reclaim the former Spanish provinces of Sardinia and Sicily, both torn from the "seamless garment" of Spanish possessions by the Allies. Over these "Lost Provinces" her current and future offspring might rule as independent monarchs.

Felipe, deep in a bout of lethargic melancholia and completely dominated by his wife's ambitions, acquiesced to the grand strategy concocted by the pair of aggressive Parmegianos. Alberoni, an energetic logistician as well as a master chef, managed to assemble an invasion force consisting of several hundred vessels bearing 33,000 troops, 8,000 horses, hundreds of cannon and other armaments, under the command of the Marquis of Lede. On June 17, 1717, this armada, said to be the largest in Spanish history, sailed for points unknown—acknowledged by everyone to be the Sicilian coast.

The perilousness inherent in the enterprise now drove the fragile Felipe into one of his increasingly bizarre manic fits. Nightly, during the first few hours of restless sleep, he tore at his cheeks with his fingernails, waking to a pillow soaked in blood. Unknown bodily secretions produced a weird phosphorescent effect: his pajamas and sheets were suffused with an eerie glow that no amount of vigorous laundering could wash away. More than once he flung himself from his bloody, neon bedding, seized a sword and ran around the palace screaming "Murder, murder!" at the top of his lungs—until subdued by specially appointed guards.

Meanwhile, Spanish troops occupied both Sardinia and Sicily unopposed. Suddenly it seemed that a reinvigorated Spanish empire loomed—or its consequence, a new bloody pan-European war.

11.

On August 11, 1718, in the choppy wine-dark seas off Cape Passaro, Sicily, the Spanish and British fleets encountered each other in a naval battle that can only be called decisive. Buoyed by the spirit of optimism emanating in ripples from the new Queen, Alberoni— now promoted Spain's First Minister—had already sent a letter warning the British to prepare for a humiliating defeat. Such letters are, in hindsight, perhaps better not sent.

Admiral Sir George Byng, commander of the British fleet, was one of those supremely confident professional military men who appear again and again throughout Britain's vigorous eighteenth century. The son of a bankrupt country squire, he had been, as he put it "raised in the King's service," entering the navy as a "King's Letter Boy"—that is, on a sort of naval scholarship—at the age of fourteen. Over the following decades, rising through the ranks, he fought pirates off the Malabar Coast, served in North Africa, the West Indies, the Baltic, and with distinction during the War of Spanish Succession. Under the command of the euphoniously named Admiral Sir Clowdesley Shovell, he participated in the defeat of the French fleet at Vigo Bay in 1702. For his services thwarting a Spanish-backed attempt to place the Stuart pretender James on the throne of Great

Britain, he was knighted and given "a diamond ring of great value" by King George I, who succeeded Queen Anne in 1714.

Now, at Cape Passaro, the Spanish, confident of victory, fired the first shots—or so the British later claimed. And in the engagement that followed, they put the lie to Spanish ambitions: "Sir, We have taken and destroyed all the Spanish ships and vessels which were upon the coast," read a typically terse dispatch from Captain George Walton, one of Byng's sub-commanders. These few words concealed a multitude of seaborne horrors: witheringly accurate British cannon fire; nearly six thousand Spanish sailors and marines killed, captured, or drowned; dozens of Spanish warships set on fire and sunk or, in a few cases, deliberately run aground by their despairing captains.

The conflict known as the War of the Quadruple Alliance had begun. It wouldn't last long, but does presage some of the geopolitics that lead to the War of Jenkins' Ear. Here's the war in brief outline: Spanish and Allied forces—this time France, Great Britain, the Netherlands, and Austria united against Spain—engaged at sea and on battlefields in both the old world and the new. Britain and France invaded Spain. Isabela, wearing a dashing blue and silver uniform custom made in Paris and sporting two large pistols, put herself at the head of a Spanish regiment at the front. Meanwhile, Spain invaded Scotland in support of the Jacobite rising only to be defeated at the Battle of Glen Shiel in 1719; the French captured Pensacola, Florida, preempting a planned Spanish invasion of South Carolina. In all these arenas Spanish arms met with failure—but none so devastating as the initial defeat at Cape Passaro, where the British Navy showed itself to be the most potent military force in the world. In other words, Alberoni and Queen Isabela's grand strategies were utterly thwarted for the moment.

"Human schemes unaided by Divine Providence are of little use," Alberoni shrugs wistfully in his *Memoires*. "The plans I devised—had but one of them been successful—would have been enough to upset the enemy's designs."

He died many years later in Piacenza at age eighty-eight, a cardinal of the Catholic Church, vastly wealthy, the honored founder of a seminary for poor boys which still bears his names. Admired for his audacity and clever stratagems by Voltaire and Frederick the Great, among others, Alberoni remains an exemplar of the adage that a scoundrel who lives long enough becomes respectable, or, in his case, an elder statesmen.

As with many eighteenth-century conflicts, when the War of the Quadruple Alliance ended in 1720 and the cannons fell silent, not much had changed. Only the South Sea Company had suffered any really serious losses—and these to the bottom line. Their profits depended on peaceful trade with Spain. Just a few years before, they had established their factories in the Spanish-American colonies at great expense. After the Battle of Cape Passaro, these factories were seized by Spain, along with all Company goods and all ships flying the Union Jack in Spanish harbors. Up to that point, the Company had made a good faith effort to turn a profit from the "legitimate" slave trade and the infrequent permission ships bearing the allowable tonnage of trade goods to Spanish-America.

The war finished what historians, fond of such labels, define as the "first period" of the *Asiento*, 1715–1718. Losses for the South Sea Company would grow to the hundreds of thousands of pounds by the time peace returned with the Treaty of the Hague in 1720. According to its terms, Felipe V and Queen Isabela, expansionist dreams defeated, withdrew Spanish troops from both Sardinia and Sicily—later swapped by Austria and Savoy—and abandoned for the time being any claims to her former possessions on Italian peninsula; Felipe dismissed Alberoni from his service—a prerequisite demanded by the victors who feared the cardinal's political acumen—and reaffirmed Spain's pledge to abandon any claims on the French throne, as already specified in the Treaty of Utrecht; French and British armies withdrew from Northern Spain; Pensacola was returned a smoking ruin to Spain by the French.

For Spain and her allies, the European balance of power had moved only slightly, like a glacier sliding inch by inch to the sea. For the South Sea Company—as shall be seen—the shift was seismic.

12.

Sometime in late 1719, the directors of the South Sea Company looked across the English Channel to France and their hearts filled with both envy and alarm: a roguish Scottish speculator, gambler, duelist, and financial maverick named John Law had formed, in conjunction with the French government, a trading company similar to the South Sea. Its goal was to both alleviate the national debt and develop France's newly acquired territory in Louisiana.

In August 1717, acting on authority granted him by Philippe d'Orleans, the pleasure-loving Regent of France, Law organized the Mississippi Company, another public-private partnership along the lines of England's South Sea Company, and like that speculative entity, based on a chimera: against the immeasurable riches sure to accrue to France from the as yet unfounded Louisiana colony, Law issued stock at 500 livres per share. He hoped to raise a million livres on the initial offering, all of which would be spent at his discretion on the establishment of a permanent French settlement in the Mississippi Valley. This settlement would repay the Mississippi Company's stockholders by becoming a prosperous colony and thus drive up share prices. The French nation immediately went speculation mad, never mind that *la Louisiane* remained a swampy, hurricane-prone, inhospitable place full of mosquitoes and Indian tribes reluctant to accept the benefits of French civilization. The value of Law's Mississippi stock rose a thousand percent in a period of months; the world's first true financial bubble was born. Law had meanwhile taken complete control of the French economy.

"You must henceforth consider Law as the First Minister," wrote Lord Stair, the British ambassador in Paris, "whose daily discourse is, that he will raise France to a greater height than ever she was, upon the ruin of England." If Law and the French could make so much money by selling stock which supposedly derived its value from as yet unrealized profits sourced in the wilderness of Louisiana, why couldn't the South Sea company make the same kind of money off their own less-than-lucrative trade with the Spanish colonies—which surely, someday soon *must* turn a profit?

"It must have been clear to the directors," Sperling comments, "that financial manipulations were less problematic, less trouble and more profitable than the *Asiento* trade. It is small wonder that they concentrated on these activities when their trade was closed down by war in 1718."

The shady stockjobbers involved with the foundation of Harley's South Sea Company decided to follow Law's example and expand the business of the Company into a purely financial arena. The original speculators—Blunt, Sawbridge, Caswall, and Turner—now expanded their cabal to include the Company treasurer, Robert Knight, and government figures like James Craggs, the postmaster general, and his son James Craggs the Younger, of the Foreign Office. But Blunt's greatest coup was convincing John Aislabie, the new chancellor of the Exchequer to join their scheme. "When one considers the career and characters of Blunt, Sawbridge, and Caswell," Sperling asserts, "the union with Aislabie and Craggs meant the project was in really dangerous hands."

Nor, in all likelihood, would their manipulations be restrained by Parliament. The Tory ruling party had been swept out of power with the death of the previous monarch, Queen Anne. Harley had been forced into retirement after a stay in the Tower upon the accession of the Whig-supported German king from Hanover—George I. The next few decades would belong to the Whigs and their able minister, Robert Walpole. A massive figure both physically and politically, brash, rude, and powerful, Walpole weighed by some estimates, more than twenty stone, which is to say more than three hundred pounds. He was also—so his enemies charged—personally corrupt.

The apotheosis of the stockjobbers had now arrived. Hardly a voice was raised against the wave of ruinous speculation that would soon inundate England.

13.

"It was while Law's plan was at its greatest height of popularity, while people were crowding in thousands to the Rue Quincampoix and ruining themselves with frantic eagerness, that the South Sea directors laid before Parliament their famous plan for paying off the national debt."

So begins Charles Mackay's account of the financial disaster that became known as the South Sea Bubble, in his seminal volume *Extraordinary Popular Delusions and the Madness of Crowds*, one of the first studies of crowd behavior and mass hysteria, published in 1841. (Among skeptical essays on fortune tellers, magnetizers, witch hunters, alchemists, and other quacks, Mackay pauses to examine the emergence and spread of urban slang, which he sees as "one of the popular follies of great cities." One expression, "What a shocking bad hat!" made the rounds of London society circa 1820 before fading out a decade or so later. Like many other slangy refrains, its original meaning—that the person at whom it was aimed wore a really awful hat—expanded over time. Eventually the phrase came to be used as a general exclamation of surprise or derision in any number of circumstances. In the opinion of this writer, it begs for a revival!)

Mackay, however, reserves his greatest scorn for the perpetrators and victims of the South Sea Bubble, which burst over England in 1720, as he put it, "when knavery gathered a rich harvest from cupidity . . . and both suffered when the day of reckoning came."

John Blunt, who "had been following Law's activities with particular interest" emerges as the chief culprit of the debacle. Blunt possessed all of Law's slipperiness, with none of that Scotsman's charm or brilliance. A Baptist, fond of quoting Scripture and urging others to live the virtuous life he failed to live himself, he came from artisan stock: his father had been a shoemaker in Rochester. Blunt began his professional life as a public letter writer in London's Birkin Lane, where he wrote letters for the illiterate for a few shillings and performed minor legal services. Extremely thrifty, he managed to save enough from his penny-ante business to set himself up as a moneylender, for which activity he charged usurious rates. This blatant loansharking enabled Blunt to build up enough of a fortune to indulge his primary passion—the creation of joint stock companies, that is corporations of like-minded investors who hoped to profit off a variety of business or improvement schemes.

Blunt's two major enterprises in pre–South Sea days (a linen cloth manufacturer and a wacky sort of aqueduct on wheels intended to provide fresh water to London) ended in losses for all stockholders involved except one, Blunt himself. He had escaped with a small fortune from both failed enterprises, and with these failures had somehow established a reputation as a businessman of great ability.

A contemporary portrait of Blunt shows a vigorous man, of forty or so, dressed in a conservatively styled but expensive looking coat, his silver-curled periwig artfully arranged. But it is his expression—confident, smug—that strikes the viewer.

"Burly and overbearing, glib, ingenious and determined to get on," writes one biographer, Blunt was "well fitted to make his way in the business jungle. . . . In the techniques of his profession, he was unequaled, and his coarse character contained just the trace of titanism which was to carry him for a moment or two to the summit of politics and finance." Or, in the words of another: "Blunt was a short, plump, unscrupulous little man who loved the feel and manipulation of money." Both these descriptions fail to include the fierce confidence caught by the portraitist; an attitude without which any eighteenth-century "Projector" (speculator) could not prosper.

Blunt's confidence at last earned him a place among the directors of the South Sea Company, which in turn led to an upwardly mobile match with the daughter of a former governor of Bengal. His new wife, an awkward woman named Susannah Cradock, had already outlived two husbands. Uncomfortable at the levees and parties her husband's financial prominence would soon necessitate, she eagerly sought the background as he rose through glittering layers of society to a baronetcy.

14.

In direct emulation of Law's Mississippi scheme then at the height of its maniacal popularity in France, Blunt proposed that the South Sea Company absorb the entire national debt of Great Britain, which amounted to £51,300,000. This sum mostly consisted of "terminable annuities," money lent to the state by private citizens in return for which they would receive a fixed yearly income for life. Blunt explained matters thusly to the astonished South Sea board: The South Sea Company would receive interest at 5 percent for ten years on money they loaned to cover the debt, which would thereafter be reduced to 4 percent. The government could only benefit from this arrangement, Blunt asserted, as the Company would additionally pay £3,500,000 outright for the privilege of lifting the debt off the nation's shoulders. But what would the Company get out of the arrangement? the directors asked.

"The advantages hoped for by the Company were much greater though not equally obvious," answers the editors of the *Britannica*'s venerable 11th Edition.

> The aim of the Directors was to persuade the annuitants of the state to exchange their annuities for South Sea stock. The stock would be issued at a high premium and thus a large amount of annuities would be purchased and extinguished by the issue of a comparatively small amount of stock.

The scheme as perfected by Blunt was poorly understood by the Whig ministers who for the moment held the reins of government: the "Two Earls" Lords Sunderland and Stanhope. The aloof Sunderland, an unfortunate choice for First Lord of the Treasury, disdained all financial matters as beneath his dignity. He had already passed on most of his duties to the decidedly unaristocratic John Aislabie, who had been a merchant associated with the Baltic trade (herring, timber, salt, and other unexciting commodities) and whom he had made chancellor of the Exchequer based on an ability to sell quantities of smoked fish to the English public.

Aislabie at first didn't quite grasp Blunt's purpose when the speculator presented his new South Sea scheme at a private meeting in January 1720. Aislabie was, asserts a historian of the Bubble, "a sly . . . basically stupid Yorkshireman." But after Blunt slowly explained the details, Aislabie, "startled" by its magnitude, suggested a smart adjustment: the Company would only subsume that portion of government debt owed to private investors, bringing the amount covered down to about £30,000,000. Adjustment made, Aislabie, satisfied, offered his critical support.

Par value of South Sea Company stock now stood at £100 per share. Should Parliament agree to the debt conversion Blunt's plan stipulated, it must also agree to allow for the creation of an equal amount of new stock, which the Company could then sell to the annuitants and other members of the general public. Word of Blunt's plan leaked out across the coffee houses of Exchange Alley and South Sea Stock quickly rose to £128. It was a nice bump but not substantial enough for Blunt's purposes. Financial historian and journalist Virginia Cowles explains it best:

> Blunt saw a chance for millions of pounds of profit, not only for the Company, but for private individuals as well . . . if Parliament agreed to the taking over of the national debt it would authorize the Company to strike £100 of new stock for every £100 of debt converted. . . . But suppose that the market price rose to £300. If an individual holding £1,200 of Government securities wanted to convert them to South Sea stock, the Company would be allowed to issue 12 new shares at £100 each. But it would only have to give the creditor four of those shares if the market price was £300. It would then have 8 surplus shares for sale, which would bring it a profit of £2,400.

The success of this scheme depended on the continual inflation of South Sea stock in a limitless bull market—and Parliament's approval.

Blunt had meanwhile received regular news from France regarding Law's publicity campaigns to artificially boost the value of

Mississippi stock—troupes of friendly dancing Indians imported from America; the forced public marriages of convicts and prostitutes to be transported for the peopling of Louisiana; extravagantly illustrated real estate brochures extolling the virtues of bayou living. Similar shenanigans, he believed, wouldn't work in England, the English being naturally less credulous and more obstinate than the French. Blunt now decided on a simple, straight-forward Anglo-Saxon tactic: bribery. And he dreamed up a bold, dastardly plan to bribe with cash or stock every member of Parliament who might be bribable. This included, as it turned out, most of that august body and the king's ministers. (One notable exception was Lord Stanhope, notorious for his incorruptibility in a corruptible age. Stanhope had recently turned down a substantial payment of £40,000 offered by the French minister Dubois for signing a treaty he was going to sign anyway. Dubois found himself utterly baffled by the earl's integrity, and even though he'd secured Stanhope's signature for free, regarded his diplomatic mission a failure.)

At Aislabie's suggestion, Blunt kicked off his bribery campaign with Mr. James Craggs, a man of humble origins, called the Elder, to distinguish himself from his son, James Craggs the Younger. Blunt's first interview with Craggs Sr. proved instantly successful. He easily recruited the postmaster, thus adding two to his conspiracy to bribe Parliament, for the son would always follow the father's lead. Moving in aristocratic circles not open to his father, however, Craggs the Younger brought valuable insight unavailable to the older men: the king's German mistresses must also be bribed, he insisted, their cooperation essential to securing the cooperation of the king, himself. He suggested £10,000 each in South Sea stock as a comfortable amount.

The mistresses—Madame Schulenburg, later Duchess of Kendall and Baroness van Kielmansegge—were dubbed the "Maypole" and the "Elephant" respectively by a contemptuous English public and often heckled when they took their carriages through the streets of London. As their unflattering nicknames infer, one was tall and gangly, the other obese, neither attractive: "The lower orders expect the King to have mistresses," observed a wag, "but not ugly ones." Ugly or not, because they had hold of the king's ear and other parts of his anatomy, they possessed a kind of power beyond that wielded by mere cabinet ministers.

Gifts of stock offered and received (including smaller contributions to Madame Kielmansegge's nieces), it now only remained to get on with the bribing of Parliament itself.

15.

Blunt and Craggs divided the nation's legislative body between them and went to work. More than a hundred MPs secretly accepted the indemnities offered; the king himself, already made honorary governor of the Company had previously received a substantial sum for his patronage. Now, under the influence of his mistresses, he gave his tacit approval as a new South Sea Bill, authorizing the conversion of government debt, rumbled through Parliament. In November 1719, the king had given a speech to the assembled members regarding the debt issue, pointing toward his acquiescence. Because the Hanoverian monarch could not speak English, it had been read out by a herald.

"We must desire you to turn your thoughts to all proper means of lessening the debts of the nation . . ." the herald began, a speech both written and delivered by others as the king sat by, bored.

At last, on January 22, 1720, Chancellor Aislabie proposed the South Sea Company's scheme to convert £30,000,000 into stock to a legislature that had been thoroughly bribed to overlook any deficiencies in the idea. Having said his piece, Aislabie sat down to silence.

"Our great men lookt as if thunderstruck, and one of them in particular turned as pale as my cravate," observed Thomas Broderick, MP, present on that day. The House of Commons had apparently been thrown into a kind of existential shock. After a quarter of an hour's muttering, according to Broderick, a heated debate ensued, pitting Tory against Whig, with much gesticulating and raised voices. It was all for show; the bribes had done their work: in the end, the House of Commons passed the South Sea Act by 172 votes to 55 on March 23, 1720.

The House of Lords, which received the Act for debate on April 7, gave it a far cooler welcome. Lord North, observed that it was "calculated for the enriching of a few and the impoverishment of a great many; and not only made for, but countenanced and authorized the fraudulent and pernicious practice of stockjobbing, which produced irreparable mischief in diverting the genius of the people from trade and industry." The rakish, unstable Philip, Duke of Wharton, from experience an expert in moral turpitude (he had recently seduced Walpole's teenage sister) called the South Sea Company "dangerous bait, which might decoy many unwary people to their ruin and allure them by a false prospect of gain to part with what they had got by their labour and industry to purchase imaginary riches."

Such were the objection of aristocrats—though none strenuous enough to delay passage. Votes had been bought, even in the upper house, even among the most illustrious and oldest names in England. Yes, Walpole had stood against the bill in the House, but with fingers crossed behind his back: he was a personal friend of the king's mistress, Madame Schulenberg, who had herself been among the first bribed. And Walpole, himself—never above an emolument—had been greased with under-the-table gifts of South Sea Stock.

Few would remember the objections of the lords, which in retrospect ring out like a prophecy, as the South Sea Bubble rose, glittering, iridescent, over the crowded coffeehouses of Exchange Alley, over the murky, refuse-strewn Thames.

16.

In England in March 1720, everyone, even those who should have known better remained dazzled by the prospects of Law's unearned millions. This even though the Mississippi Bubble had already burst, sending the French nation into financial ruin and Law into exile. Almost everyone involved with the South Sea scheme failed to see the coming apocalypse, the reflection of their fate in the Mississippi Company's dizzying sudden decline. Even Craggs the Younger, who had been informed of the particulars of the Mississippi disaster by Lord Stair, refused to believe such a thing could happen in England. The South Sea Act had just been bought and paid for and passed. The nation held its breath. And the great swindle began.

Though the government had stipulated that the Company might manufacture only one share of stock per every £100 of privatized debt, Blunt offered twenty thousand "unconverted" shares on April 20, 1720. This offering, technically illegal, went unchallenged by Parliament and generally unexamined in the London press. Everyone wanted a piece of South Sea action and the stock sold out in a single afternoon. Blunt somehow managed to oversell by two-and-a-half thousand shares, claiming that the tumult at South Sea House, where the shares were offered, had prevented the Company's two recording clerks, set up at opposite ends of the main gallery, from communicating with each other. But the same "accidental" overselling occurred at the next stock offering, also illegal, with an additional five thousand shares oversubscribed. Again, no one complained; no legal actions were contemplated.

The buying and selling of stock quickly became a national mania. In just a few weeks England's first stock market boom had taken hold and instantly began to exhibit Mississippi-style excesses.

"Sensible men beheld the extraordinary infatuation of the people with sorrow and alarm," Mackay writes. "England presented a singular spectacle. The public mind was in a state of unwholesome fermentation. Men were no longer satisfied with the slow but sure profits of a cautious industry. The hope of boundless wealth for the morrow made them heedless and extravagant." Though there were still "some both in and out of Parliament who foresaw clearly the ruin that was impending. Mr. Walpole did not cease his gloomy forebodings."

However, these forebodings did not prevent Walpole and others from continuing to invest heavily in South Sea stock. Even ladies raced to join the stockjobbing game—unheard of before the boom, when the coffeehouses had been off-limits to anyone wearing a petticoat. Exchange Alley had lately come to resemble a fashionable brothel, frequented by ladies of quality but also by actresses and whores, as described by a waggish newspaper poet of the day:

> *Our greatest ladies hither come*
> *And ply in chariots daily;*
> *Oft pawn their jewels for a sum*
> *To venture in the Alley.*
> *Young harlots too from Drury Lane*
> *Approach the Change in coaches*
> *To fool away the gold they gain*
> *By their impure debauches.*

Stockjobbing fever soon spread from aristocrats and *demimondaines* to just about everyone else, as catchable as smallpox or gin-induced alcoholism, two other scourges of eighteenth-century London. Warned an editorialist of the popular *Weekly Journal* on March 26, 1720:

> 'Tis said that abundance of our country gentlemen and rich farmers are upon the roads from several parts of the Kingdom, all expecting no less than to ride down again every man in his coach and six; but if a friend's advice is worth anything, let them take care, for though there are some prizes, they may find many more blanks, and they may happen to lose all that in an hour in Exchange Alley, which the industry and care of their ancestors has been scraping together for some ages.

In an era addicted to gambling, when the gentry wagered and lost thousands nightly at London's gaming tables, the buying and selling of stock had become just another addiction. According to the law, joint stock companies required royal permission in the form of a charter to open their doors to trade. Now, as April warmed to May, dozens of new companies, modeling themselves on the South Sea, offered their stock to speculators, without the requisite charter. These "Bubble Companies," touted a variety of moneymaking ventures, a few legitimate, most laughable, some bizarre, all illegal. Selected from a list of eighty-six such companies provided by Mackay, we have the following:

For importing a large number of jackasses from Spain to improve the breed of British Mules.

For building ships against pirates.

For insuring all masters and mistresses against the losses they may sustain by servants.

For a wheel of perpetual motion. Capital one million.

For an immediate expeditious and cleanly manner of emptying necessary houses throughout England at a cost of L2,000,000.

For insuring marriage against divorce.

For trading in hair.

For effectively settling the islands of Blanco and Sal Tartagus.

For improving malt liquors. Capital, four millions.

For insuring horses.

For the transmutation of quicksilver (mercury) into a malleable fine metal.

Though, arguably, some fine investment opportunities might be found on the partial list above—who wouldn't for example, want to insure marriage against divorce or purchase top-quality human hair?—most ventured into the territory of fraud: a London printer offered stock in a company "for carrying on an undertaking of Great Advantage but no one knows what it is." He sold a thousand shares of this phantom company for two pounds each on the first day. That night he wisely packed up and decamped for the Continent.

These and similar enterprises inspired another London printer to devise a pack of satirical Bubble Playing Cards, each card depicting an absurd company not so different from the real thing: one card touted the manufacture of "Puckle's Machine Gun," which could discharge both round and square cannonballs—the former designed to destroy Christians, the latter Turks; another "for an engine to move the South Sea House to Moorgate"; yet another "for the melting down of sawdust chips and casting them into clean deal boards, without cracks or knots."

A full set of these cards still exists in the British Museum; copies may be had in the museum shop. Play them at your own risk.

17.

The bubble inflated daily through the spring and summer of 1720. With the South Sea Company leading the way: share price rose to £400 by early May, then to £550 by the end of the month. June saw a rise to £890; in July it touched £1000. Still, the avaricious Blunt who had lately become—after the manner of Law in Paris—one of the most sought-after figures in London society, resented the illegal Bubble Companies. He believed they siphoned investors' money that would otherwise go to the South Sea. In March, he had persuaded Parliament to open an investigation into them. Results became known on June 11: the illegal Bubble Companies would be suppressed—though investors couldn't quite believe this would happen. Wasn't everyone happily making money?

The weather in London in July grew miserably hot. No one paid any attention to the rioting that had broken out in France. Sweating in his expensive velvets, Blunt took his wife and family on vacation to the spa at Tunbridge Wells. Publicly he exuded his usual confidence in the limitless potential of South Sea stock; privately he gave the bubble till November, around Guy Fawkes Day. The prudent should "withdraw" by then.

Like a soldier who knows he will be killed in the next battle and whose sad presentiment comes true, the directors of the Company also felt it coming. Members of the Company's "inner circle" agreed with Blunt; meanwhile the national debt of England, supposedly converted by the Company's stock, hadn't been converted at all. As Law had printed increasingly worthless paper money to cover the French debt, the Company had manufactured more stock and offered credit to those who wished to purchase more—against the value of the stock to be purchased. Thousands jumped at this opportunity. It was a financial Ouroboros, a paper snake eating its own tail. Blunt made fifty thousand more shares available at £1000 per share, bumping share price another £50—though everyone had expected a larger boost from the extravagant offering. Suddenly, even the smallest investor could hear the bubble creaking as it slid imperceptibly earthward.

Blunt had left London for Tunbridge Wells a wealthy man, admired by all and no longer a commoner—the king, mightily pleased by his profit of £86,000 had knighted him before departing for Hanover. The pinprick that exploded the bubble came inadvertently from Blunt himself: in mid-August, Parliament at last took action against the multitude of Bubble Companies declared illegal in June at Blunt's insistence and shut them down. Those investors who had bought shares in these companies lost everything they had invested. Now, many set about selling South Sea shares to cover their losses, which immediately launched a frenzy of panic selling.

"Various are the conjectures why the South Sea directors have suffered the cloud to break so early," wrote MP Thomas Broderick, who would eventually demand a parliamentary investigation into the affair. "I made no doubt but they would do so when they found it to their advantage. They have stretched credit so far beyond what it would bear, that specie proves insufficient to support it. Their most considerable men have drawn out, securing themselves by the losses of the deluded, thoughtless numbers, whose understandings have been overruled by avarice and the hope of making mountains out of molehills. The consternation is inexpressible—rage beyond description, and the case altogether so desperate, that I do not see any plan or scheme so much as thought of for averting the blow."

On August 17, South Sea share price stood at £1000; a month later share price had fallen to £190. Financial disaster had come to England. The resulting crash, easily as dire as the New York Stock

Market Crash of 1929 or the US Housing Bubble Crisis of 2008, obtained the same results: mass bankruptcies, social unrest, suicides.

Craggs the Elder took an overdose of opium in the Tower, where he'd been imprisoned pending investigation for bribery and financial irregularities—though this desperate act perhaps had more to do with the death of his beloved son from smallpox a few weeks earlier. Blunt and the other directors who had cynically given the bubble till November had clearly miscalculated. He now returned to London from Tunbridge Wells in haste, at the urgent request of the South Sea board. Stepping out of his new carriage into the unusually bitter heat of August, he protested sourly that "he did not know but it might have cost him his life to have left off drinking the waters so abruptly; and that he had rather given £10,000 than to have come up to town."

In the end, it would cost him—and England—much, much more than ten thousand pounds.

18.

When the dust had settled, those ruined by the South Sea Bubble cried out for revenge. Parliment divided itself in two general factions. The first, led by Walpole proposed a government bailout of the South Sea Company, of which the king was governor and his mistresses major shareholders. The second fumed and vented, calling the South Sea directors "plunderers of the nation" and "parricides of their country." These advocated jail time and even execution for the perpetrators. The astute Walpole, aware that many in Parliament had benefited from South Sea speculations, including himself, sought a middle course: in this, he acted—so said the pamphleteers—as a "skreen" between the guilty and the justice they deserved, earning himself the unenviable title of "Skreenmaster General." The guilty they inferred, hid themselves behind his massive bulk.

Walpole nevertheless steered the nation away from revolution and riot and managed to preserve the status quo. The government and king must be maintained despite all the bankruptcies and fraud. A percentage of South Sea Company debts would be paid from the nation's general fund, while major perpetrators would be punished though the confiscation of their estates and fortunes. The directors of the South Sea Company were on the whole harshly treated. Mandates handed down by a parliamentary "secret committee" chaired by Broderick, resulted in their sacking and the collection of over two million pounds in fines. Most of them were left with enough to live on, squeaking out meager allowances, depending on degree of culpability.

Blunt was left with £1000 and ten times that amount of personal disgrace, but escaped a threatened term in prison. He retired to Bath in comfort, living off an allowance provided by his son, one of those few who had made a tidy sum in the Bubble. Edward Gibbon, grandfather of the author of *Decline and Fall of the Roman Empire*, a prominent South Sea board member, was allowed £10,000 out of a personal fortune of over £100,000:

"On these ruins," commented the historian in his memoirs, "with the skill and credit, of which Parliament had not been able to despoil him, my grandfather at a mature age erected the edifice of a new fortune."

In other words, through ingenuity or connections, the rich generally manage to avoid incarceration and stay rich. The same can be said of those reckless speculators behind the US Housing Bubble Crisis of 2008.

Alexander Pope wrote the South Sea Bubble's epitaph:

At length corruption, like a general flood
Did deluge all, and avarice creeping on
Spread like a low-born mist and hid the sun.

Statesmen and patriots plied alike these stocks,
Peeress and butler shared alike the box,
And judges jobbed and bishops bit the town,
And mighty dukes packed cards for half-a-crown—
Britain lay sunk in lucre's sordid charms.

Walpole, who had sold his South Sea stock at the exact right moment, emerged from the disaster with his fortune intact and unexamined, and his political power solidified. He became "First Minister" in April 1722 and is considered by historians as England's first true Prime Minister—a post he held for the next twenty years, a period of Whig ascendancy, increasing prosperity, and no major wars. England was a trading nation and trade was good. Why should the nation not recover robustly from a brief, sharp financial escapade that had ended badly?

The South Sea Company, with the aid of Walpole, escaped dissolution. With new directors and a renewed mission, it resumed its operations under the *Asiento de Negros* for which it had been designed—that is, trading slaves to the Spanish American colonies, augmented by the proceeds of the annual ships. Unfortunately, with this formula, as everyone knew, no money could be made. The slave trade and the meager profits off a single cargo-load of manufactured goods could not long sustain the shareholders' expectations of profits after the bubble burst.

A new era of smuggling—winked at by the government and Company alike—on a scale never before imagined, had begun.

John Blunt (left) South Sea Bubble (right)

THREE

The Road to Jenkins' Ear

From the 13th Siege of Gibraltar to Walpole's Lament,
1727–1739

1.

On January 1, 1727, the Marquis of Pozobueno, Spanish Ambassador to the Court of St. James, delivered a strongly worded diplomatic message to the Duke of Newcastle, Secretary of State for the Southern Department, in London. This particular diplomatic message, however, would prove anything but diplomatic. Its operative clause boiled down to a single impossible Spanish ultimatum, would lead to yet another costly and inconclusive Anglo-Spanish War, this one unimaginatively dubbed the Anglo-Spanish War of 1727–1729. His Catholic Majesty, King Felipe V of Spain demanded the immediate return of Gibraltar, which had been seized by a daring Anglo-Dutch naval operation in 1704, during the War of Spanish Succession. Never mind that Britain's possession of the famous "Rock" had been subsequently confirmed in Article X of the Treaty of Utrecht, signed by King Felipe himself.

The marquis spoke for the king (and for Queen Isabela, Spain's actual ruler, the king just then suffering from one of his manic-depressive episodes). The loss of Gibraltar had been experienced by Their Catholic Majesties as a painful amputation. It was as if a big toe had been lopped off the Mediterranean foot of Spain. In King Felipe's opinion, Britain had effectively nullified Article X by admitting into Gibraltar "the Jews and Moors, contrary to our Holy Religion," which the Article specifically forbade. More, Britain had allowed into Spain "contrabands, which are carried on to the prejudice of his Majesty's revenues." Here, Pozobueno's message identified two powerful motivations for war, close to the heart of every Spaniard: religion and gold.

At the conclusion of the *Reconquista* in 1492, Spain had forcibly expelled its Jewish and Moorish populations from the Iberian Peninsula. The last of them left from Gibraltar for North Africa that notable year. Spain's Holy Soil had long been purified of these twin scourges; she would not now suffer their return under British auspices. And, as usual with the British, smuggling had become the major occupation of her traders in Gibraltar. The years between 1704 and 1727 had seen a glut of British manufactured goods weaseled around the neck of the isthmus into Spain in exchange for gold and raw materials.

Pozobueno's message was in effect a declaration of war. To Spain, Gibraltar and smuggling were the chief causes, but other issues lurked in the background, having to do with the European balance of power so precious to the eighteenth-century strategic mind.

Spain had once again made common cause with Austria, her old Hapsburg ally, this union sealed by the Treaty of Vienna in

1725. In the terms of this treaty lurked Spain's recognition of the controversial "Pragmatic Sanction" which would allow the Austrian Emperor Charles's daughter Maria-Theresa to inherit the throne and the Imperial title. Spain also recognized the new Austrian "Ostend Company" and gave it leave to trade with her American colonies. Britain had fought bitterly for these trading privileges, obtained by the South Sea Company after great difficulty and the blood of Malplaquet. Spain's bequest of them to an upstart Austrian trading concern could not pass without bloodshed.

Also, reportedly, a secret treaty existed, signed by Felipe and Charles, which yoked their kingdoms in an aggressive war against the rest of Europe. Their united armies would seize Alsace, Roussilon, and Navarre from France, and Gibraltar and Menorca from Britain. The secret treaty has never been located. "Secrecy in history" is a problematic thing, lying as it does halfway between fact and conspiracy. Some historians deny, others assert the existence of this shadowy document. But its existence was widely believed at the time by British diplomats and King George himself, and thus has historic merit if only for how belief in its existence motivated these key players. Thus, anxieties regarding a newly revitalized and antagonistic Spain drove King George to sign a counter-agreement, the Treaty of Hanover with France and Prussia.

It seemed the stage had been set for yet another pan-European conflict, with England and Spain on opposite sides of the chess board once again—the third time in twenty years. The lessons of Malplaquet would have to be learned all over again.

2.

For Britain, the new war with Spain would be fought on two fronts: in the West Indies and at Gibraltar. The Rock would soon undergo what is now identified as its 13th Siege. Fighting began on February 22, 1727 with an exchange of cannon-fire between Spanish forces, led by the impetuous Count de Las Torres de Alcorrín at the head of a besieging army of 18,000 men against Gibraltar's garrison of 1,500, later reinforced by sea to 5,500. When the siege began, both the Governor of Gibraltar, Lord Portmere, and the Lieutenant Governor, Colonel Clayton were in England taking the waters, leaving command to Colonel Richard Kane, lieutenant governor of Menorca, then in Gibraltar on temporary assignment.

From the beginning, the 13th Siege was a quixotic undertaking on the part of Spain. Felipe V had been warned by his senior military advisors of the impossibility of taking the nearly impregnable rock without an overwhelming naval force supporting a massive land assault. But the Spanish Navy, destroyed at the Battle of Cape Passaro in 1718, had not yet been rebuilt. The king's advisors, the Marquis de Villadarias and a battle-hardened Flemish military engineer, the Marquis Verboom both offered carefully considered professional advice: A siege of Gibraltar, under the present circumstances, would fail. But the fiery Las Torres insisted that he could in six weeks deliver Spain from this "noxious settlement of foreigners and heretics," and called into question the patriotism and courage of anyone who disagreed with him. As is often the case, bombastic overheated rhetoric prevailed over common sense. Of course, Las Torres was short on details; no doubt soldierly *elan* and God's status as a Spanish Catholic would win the day.

The count mustered an army of thirty infantry battalions and six squadrons of cavalry; his artillery included seventy-two mortars and ninety-two cannons, along with several big siege guns brought from Cádiz. His army, though nominally Spanish, consisted mostly of foreign mercenaries whose nationalities mirrored Spain's former European possessions and her revitalized relationship with Austria: three battalions of Walloons (Flemish-speaking Belgians); three battalions of French-speaking Belgians; four battalions of Irish Jacobites (Irish Catholic supporters of the Stuart pretender to the English throne); two Savoyard battalions; two Neapolitan, one Swiss, one Corsican, and one Sicilian. A truly polyglot mixture that only presaged a series of disastrous communications breakdowns.

Serving as commander of the Irish Jacobites and as Las Torres's *aide-de-camp* was the scandalous Philip, Duke of Wharton—the English peer who had seduced Walpole's sister. Despite his own good advice, he had been ruined by reckless speculation during the South Sea Bubble and, pursued by his creditors, had turned against King George and fled the country to fight for Spain. Brilliant, dissolute, when sober a canny politician and eloquent pamphleteer, he was unfortunately most often drunk. His wild antics had even managed to scandalize an age used to alcoholic escapades and aristocratic excesses. Alexander Pope called Wharton "the scorn and wonder of our days." He was, the poet said, a walking paradox, a man "too rash for thought, for action too refined." In England, Wharton had been one of the founders of the infamous Hellfire Club, a secret society open to iconoclastic, hard-living aristocrats. Among other picturesque debaucheries they indulged in blasphemous parodies of Anglican religious rites, performed by naked prostitutes.

The death of Wharton's young son from smallpox in 1720 threw him into the arms of his worst impulses and caused a rupture with his first wife—his last link to what might be called normal life. More than £120,000 in debt—an astronomical sum, the modern equivalent of tens of millions—Wharton first sought refuge in Italy. There, he had offered his services to the Pretender, James III, who ran a tinsel parallel court in Rome. The exiled Stuart, impressed with Wharton's energy and title, awarded him the coveted Order of the Garter, which only the rightful King of England could bestow.

The rogue duke's abandoned first wife died—some say from drink, others from despair—and he married again in Spain, the beautiful daughter of an Irish soldier who was one of Queen Isabela's maids of honor. At the wedding, Wharton, drunk as usual, exposed his penis—apparently of an impressive size—to the assembled company, just to show what his wife "would have this night buried in her gutts."

By the time Wharton reached the Spanish lines at Gibraltar, he had become an embarrassment. Perpetually drunk, and with no previous military experience, he led suicidal charges straight at the British fortifications, daring the soldiers of his own country to fire at him: "whereupon the soldiers," wrote an early twentieth-century biographer, "being far from desirous to kill a madcap nobleman of their own nation held their fire and suffered him to return uninjured to his trenches."

But Wharton's bravado eventually caught up with him. As an eyewitness reported:

> The day before yesterday, the Duke of Wharton insisted on going to a Battery to show his Garter-Riband, crying out a thousand times "Long Live the Pretender," and using a quantity of bad language. They represented to him repeatedly that he ought to withdraw, but he refused to do so. At last, he was struck by a piece of shell on the toe. He had been drinking Brandy, otherwise perhaps he would have been wiser.

This injury, significant enough to lead military surgeons to contemplate the amputation of his foot, sufficed to invalid the Duke out of active service. Shortly thereafter, Parliament declared him an outlaw and confiscated his estates and property in England. A few years later, broke, drunk-sick, and sick at heart, the one-time roguish bon vivant, nursed by his long-suffering second wife, died in the Royal Cistercian Monastery at Poblet in Spain. He lies there still, buried beneath a crumbling, vine-covered slab, its inscription barely legible.

3.

The 13th Siege of Gibraltar dragged on, measured in the parabola of each falling cannon ball.

The Count de Las Torres pounded British fortifications with his artillery to no avail. Many of his guns, poorly cast, "drooped at the mouth" from overheating or burst after repeated use. Attempts at undermining also failed. Spanish miners clambered up the cliff face to dig a gallery large enough to contain four hundred barrels of gunpowder. They endured withering fire from a British naval squadron riding the bay below but it was the tough fiber of the rock and not British guns that ultimately doomed their effort: the hard granite of Gibraltar refused to yield to Spanish pickaxes. To mine a gallery of sufficient size, Spanish engineers estimated, would take eight-to-ten months of constant labor. The plan was abandoned after several fruitless weeks and many pointless casualties.

Meanwhile, in the battered town of Gibraltar, the usual drama played out: rationing, sickness, cruel punishments meted out to deserters, hoarders, thieves, profiteers, and anyone else who violated the rules of behavior during a state of siege. Time passed slowly between the nearly unendurable cannonades of what one participant dubbed a "gunner's war," in which the danger of being killed by one's own guns exploding was as great as being killed by enemy fire. Two British officers committed suicide out of sheer ennui, another was killed in a duel. In April, torrential rains made life miserable for the defenders and for the besiegers, whose zig-zag trenches, inexorably approaching, filled with mud. Then the days grew long and hot; bodies stank in the rubble.

All the Spanish residents of Gibraltar had been expelled at the beginning of the siege, their loyalty suspect, leaving two hundred Genoese and one hundred Jews to assist the British garrison with the defense of the town. Spanish shells destroyed British fortifications daily; at night these were rebuilt with grueling effort. According to an unnamed British officer—identified only by the initials S. H.—who kept a diary of the siege, later published, the Jews at first balked at the demands of their unending labor:

"A body of the Jews desire to leave to retire to Barbary, because commanded to work for the common Preservation," S. H. observed, "but answer'd by the Governor that as they had enjoy'd safe and plenty during Peace, if they will not assist for their own safety, they shall be turned over to the Spaniard." With this rebuke, their attitude soon changed, and another siege diarist later noted "the Jews were not a little serviceable, they wrought in the most indefatigable manner and spared no pains where they could be of any advantage."

A shipment of prostitutes arrived from Ireland in mid-May, conveyed by a Royal Navy corvette for the diversion of the garrison. From these unfortunate women, came, says S. H. "a great number of necessary evils." Some of them proved not-surprisingly unruly, drinking and soliciting in the streets. By way of discipline, they were subjected to an odd contraption called the "Whirligig." The Diarist comments:

A poor lady, by name Chidley . . . was most formally conducted to a pretty Whim or Whirligig, in the form of a Bird Cage, for the greater benefit of air. It contains Room enough for one person. . . . It is fixed between two swivels, so is turned around till it makes the person, if not us'd very gently, a little giddy and Land Sick. This Office was performed by two of the private Gentlemen of the Garrison, for the space of an hour in the Market Place, being well attended. All this was to oblige her for the following good qualities, which she had the goodness to make frequent use of, such as giving soft words in smooth language, beating

better manners into several men, and a too frequent bestow-
ing of other favors.

The effect of this "whim" was actually more punishing than the
Diarist allows: after a few minutes, "the centrifugal action caused
the victim to empty through every orifice."

The cruelties of the age were not of course confined to women.
Random cannon balls took off the heads and limbs of garrison
troops. Moors, coming and going from across the straits to Africa
in small boats sold necessary provisions at exorbitant prices that
could only be afforded by officers. Two of the former, exposed as
spies in the pay of Spain, were "put to death and afterwards flayed,"
reports S. H. "Their skins were then nailed to the gates of the town,
where they appeared in the same proportions when alive, and being
large, gigantic fellows, as the Moors in general are, they were horrid
ghastly spectacles." He adds:

> The best part of them were remaining when we came away.
> Nature had sent them into the world with their hides tanned,
> so that the heat of the sun, which is very intense at Gibraltar,
> could add but little to their original dusk; but it had so hard-
> ened them that they soon seemed equally solid with the gates
> themselves. After the siege they were much lessened by the
> curiosity of our people, who cut out a great many pieces of
> them to bring to England, one of which, to gratify our readers,
> may be seen at Mr. Warner's, the publisher of this treatise.

Yellow fever, a relatively new scourge in Europe, brought on
slave ships—Gibraltar being one of the ports involved in the triangle
trade—eventually felled more than five hundred of the defenders
and an unknown but probably greater number of Spaniards, given
their position in wet, mosquito-ridden trenches.

At last, in the penultimate week of June, the Spanish bombardment ceased all at once, and the hot blue sky above the Rock, so recently ripped by cannonballs, cleared. The Count de Las Torres sent a fatted calf to the governor, Lord Portmere, long since returned from England to organize the defense. With this ironically biblical gift, Las Torres acknowledged his defeat. His remaining engineers, consulted at last, had advised him that Gibraltar could not be penetrated with the forces available, especially in the absence of naval control of the Straits. The Count's vehemence and bellicosity had failed to deliver the promised outcome. Now he blamed his chief engineer, Verboom—who he claimed had worked against him—and who had decamped weeks before to Madrid to protest to King Felipe the futility of the siege. Las Torres also blamed the poor quality of his own soldiery; most of them foreign mercenaries with more allegiance to their pay than the Spanish cause. In any case, he had been remarkably spendthrift with their lives.

The 13th Siege ended in a British victory against overwhelming odds, which only served to bolster their growing reputation as an obstinate and warlike people. The Rock would remain in British hands—as it does to this day, over Spain's unending objections. At no point during the Siege had the defenders been in any real danger of losing Gibraltar. They were, in fact, better supplied by sea from England, than the Spanish in their own country—the latter had found it necessary to bring all provisions slowly overland from Andalusia in primitive carts on rough roads. Also, fresh water ran clear and potable from various places on the Rock; the Spanish had to content themselves with barrels of water "black as a hat and stinking."

When the firing stopped, official Spanish casualties stood at 1,500 killed, 2,450 wounded, with more than 3,000 deserting to British lines; on the British side 118 killed, 207 wounded—though the numbers who succumbed to disease on both sides were no doubt far greater. According to S. H. "we begin to find our soldiers sicken very much into fluxes and gripes of the bowls, which the physicians attributed to the too frequent drinking of new wine, and a great deal of which was sour . . . the disorder of the gripes and flux"— probably dysentery and the flu—"became at length so epidemical that our hospitals were all filled with the sick, five or six of a night almost constantly dying for a considerable time together."

The siege had lasted more than four months during which 24,000 shells and 53,000 round shot had been expended: "We laughed at the Spaniards for fools," concludes the Diarist, "to throw away their Powder and Balls and Shells. . . . Thus ended the famous siege which made rather more noise in the world in preparation than when undertaken."

Meanwhile, the war continued across the Atlantic, with rather different results.

4.

Admiral Hosier's martyred ghost haunted the British imagination for generations: Wrapped in a dingy hammock, with four thousand other ghosts similarly attired at his side, all pointed spectral fingers at Robert Walpole, whose craven, short-sighted foreign policy had assured their deaths. The eighteenth-century balladeer Richard Glover memorably illustrated this spectral nightmare:

> *On a sudden, shrilly sounding*
> *Hideous yelles and shrieks were heard;*
> *Then, each heart with fears confounding*
> *A sad troop of ghosts appeared;*
> *All in dreary hammocks shrouded,*
> *Which for winding sheets they wore;*

and with looks of sorrow clouded
Frowning on that hostile shore

This stanza, plucked from Glover's lengthy ballad *Admiral Hosier's Ghost*, was written a dozen years after the Admiral perished along with his command, cruising the fetid, mosquito-infested waters off Porto Bello, entrepôt of the Spanish Treasure Fleet, on the Caribbean side of the Panamanian isthmus. The ballad from which it was taken resides among several dozen pieces collected in one of the best-selling anthologies of the era, the *English Reliques*, a volume of popular English songs and ballads, supposedly transcribed from an elusive, handwritten manuscript rescued from the fireplace at a country house: The chambermaid had been using its stiff age-spotted pages as kindling, so the story goes, until the manuscript was recognized, just in time, as a national treasure by an antiquary visiting for the weekend.

Historical consensus blames the foreign policy failures of the king and his ministers—and the Royal Navy's criminally bad hygienic practices—for Hosier's disaster. The British public at the time chiefly blamed Robert Walpole: Walpole, now the preeminent Whig, First Minister, wily politician, corrupt, corruptible, a man of business, a compromiser, a deal-maker. Trading nations, Walpole maintained, need never go to war. A deal and greater profits could solve any international problem. He was at heart, a vulgar but peaceable country gentlemen, like Squire Allworthy in Fielding's *Tom Jones*—the racy, literary masterpiece of England's mid-eighteenth century. Portraits of Walpole (now dubbed the "Great Man" by the London press, both for his size and his influence) show a hearty man of enormous bulk, always outdoors, dressed in country clothes with a couple of hunting dogs at his side, a rifle slung casually over his arm. All in all, Walpole seems to say to us across the years, "I'd rather be out huntin'." In fact, he was the preeminent politician of his era, his hunting grounds the drawing rooms and coffee houses of London.

Spain's renewed alliance with Austria and the growing problem of depredations of the *guarda costa* on British shipping in the West Indies gave Walpole a case of political indigestion. He knew a full-scale war with Spain and her allies loomed; he wished to avert it at all costs, but could not be seen as an appeaser. Spain's attack on Gibraltar would soon force his hand in the Mediterranean. Still hoping to avoid an all-out war inimical to British trading interests, his ministry dispatched a squadron to the West Indies, with the capable, doomed Rear Admiral Francis Hosier in command.

Hosier, aboard his flagship *Breda* dropped anchor off the Bastimentos Islands, near Porto Bello, Panama, on June 6, 1726. He was eventually joined by sixteen other ships serving on the Jamaica Station and a few from England, bringing his squadron up to twenty. Limited rules of engagement imposed by the Walpolian government ensured military disaster: Hosier was instructed to blockade the port city of Porto Bello, but not to make any move to take the town itself, nor any vessel riding in its harbor. His squadron, encompassing 4,750 men, would instead cruise up and down endlessly, allowing no Spanish ships to proceed without first examining their cargo for treasure. If found, this might be confiscated.

The strategists at the Admiralty knew that Spain's economy relied on the annual shipment of silver from the famous Potosi mines and other sources. Porto Bello, protected by three impressive fortresses, with its stone warehouses and garrison troops, operated as one of the chief transshipment points. Silver came up the Pacific coast by sail and across the isthmus by mule train where it met, at Porto Bello the galleons of the Spanish treasure fleet. These were laden for the final leg of the journey to Cádiz.

Hosier would seize these galleons should they emerge from their protected anchorage; if they did not emerge he would do . . . nothing. A deadly waiting game ensued. The Spanish, as it turned out, knew how to wait better than the British Navy, "forced to loiter and cruise off a mosquito-infested coast."

5.

At first, the Governor of Porto Bello pretended to be baffled by the presence of Hosier's squadron at his doorstep. He sent a carefully worded dispatch enquiring politely the reason for the blockade—as far as he knew, England and Spain were not at war. As it happened, a South Sea Company "permission ship," the *Royal George*, London-bound and laden with a rich cargo of raw materials from the Spanish colonies, lay refitting for the journey home in Porto Bello harbor. Hosier, using the *Royal George* as a pretext, informed the governor that his entire squadron had been sent as an escort for this single trading vessel. The governor quickly saw to it that the *Royal George*, loaded and ready, sailed unmolested across the bar to join its supposed escort. Of course, Hosier did not call off his blockade once the *Royal George* had sailed for home. Now, what had been painfully obvious became utterly clear: Hosier was after the treasure galleons, the economic lifeblood of Spain. Their cargos now unloaded and stored for safekeeping in Porto Bello's warehouses, the galleons still failed to emerge.

Week after week, all through the sweltering hot months of the tropics, Hosier's squadron sailed up and down, helpless to pursue their prey, tantalizingly close but untouchable. Gradually, the British sailors and officers began to sicken and die from the same yellow fever that had made a brief appearance at Gibraltar. It is a mosquito-borne tropical disease, a fast killer to which Englishmen had no resistance.

Shipboard hygiene at this period, notoriously lax, only increased the morbidity of the contagion. Sailors lived in airless galleries below decks, amid their own slops. The ships stank of feces and decay; the "iron rations" of salt pork and hardtack became rotten and vermin-infested in the tropical heat.

"It is doubtful whether any other British fleet had ever suffered from disease so severely as Hosier's suffered in 1726–1727," says naval historian William Laird Clowes in his magisterial seven-volume *The Royal Navy*. After six months of aimless cruising, officers and crew became "daily more distressed by the ravages of the epidemic" to the point where their large, complex warships could no longer be sailed properly. At last, blockade duty became impracticable, and Hosier ordered a retreat to Jamaica. Here, he hoped that he and the remains of his crew might recuperate, his vessels would be refit, and new sailors be recruited. Meanwhile, he applied desperately to the Admiralty for a release from his inhibiting orders. Porto Bello itself might be taken with a mere seven ships, he insisted, and he commanded twenty. The Admiralty's response is not recorded, but Walpole's strategy remained in place—to harass Spain up to the point of engaging her in all-out war.

What do we know of Hosier? He was a competent and courageous officer of a relatively advanced age (fifty-four) when sent by his government on the fruitless and deadly mission to Porto Bello. He had been a young lieutenant at the Battle of Barfleur in 1692—a decisive naval engagement that had prevented France from aiding the restoration of the ousted Stuart monarch, James II to England's throne. Hosier came from a naval family. His father had been a close associate of the great diarist and "Savior of the English Navy" Samuel Pepys. No portraits of Hosier exist, but we can imagine the wig rising over his forehead, the expression of steely resolve in his eye, the velvet coat with extravagant cuffs, perhaps a breastplate, as military fashion dictated, one hand on the pommel of his sword.

After a few weeks of R&R in Jamaica, Hosier returned doggedly to his blockading duties off Porto Bello, cutting a line between the Bastimentos and the Bay of Sharks. This water had always been fatal to English seamen: the renowned Sir Francis Drake had died thereabouts in 1596, aboard his famous ship the *Golden Hind*. The lead coffin bearing the remains of the famous Elizabethan pirate and circumnavigator clutching his jeweled sword still lies somewhere on the ocean floor off the Panamanian coast, the unfound Holy Grail of Caribbean sport divers.

6.

On March 10, 1727, Admiral Hosier at last surrendered to the disease that had killed so many of his men:

"His death has been attributed to anxiety and chagrin," Clowes says, "but was in fact caused by fever. Nor is it astonishing that the fleet was then little better than a floating charnel house. The most elementary prescriptions of sanitary science seem to have been neglected."

They buried Hosier, wrapped in a bit of sail cloth, in the bilge of his flagship, where no doubt, it began to stink and fester, and "where it remained, a necessary source of danger to all on board." Eventually, he was disinterred and transported aboard the ironically named vessel *Happy* for a martyr's burial in England. Unfortunately, Hosier's death did nothing to change government policy regarding the blockade. He was replaced in command by acting senior naval officer Edward St. Loe, until this gentleman was superseded by Vice-Admiral Edward Hopson, fresh from the Siege of Gibraltar. Hopson arrived at the Jamaica Station on January 29, 1726; he lasted until May 8, when he too died of yellow fever, aboard his flagship. St. Loe once again took command until—after outlasting his two superior officers, the odds caught up with him on April 22. He was buried at sea, wrapped in the Union Jack.

7.

With negotiations between Britain and Spain reaching for a temporary resolution at peace talks held at Soissons in Northern France, the mission to Porto Bello was at last called off. It had been a strategic failure. More than 4,000 of Hosier's squadron had died out of an initial strength of 4,750—including two rear admirals, eight captains and forty lieutenants. The operation had also been a tactical failure: taking advantage of Hosier's absence in Jamaica, in January 1727, the Spanish Admiral Antonio de Gaztañeta slipped through the British blockade and led the Spanish Treasure Fleet, bearing 31 million pesos worth of silver, back to Spain.

Echoes of what the British public rightly saw as a national tragedy reverberated for the next dozen years. Though Britain had not exactly lost the Anglo-Spanish War of 1727–1729 (they had retained Gibraltar against a numerically superior Spanish army) and though Spain had not exactly won the war (they had not retrieved Gibraltar from the hands of Protestant heretics), the waiting game played at the blockade of Porto Bello had essentially defeated the vaunted British Royal Navy. (This lesson would be applied by Blas de Lezo a dozen years later to greater effect.) And treasure, ripped from the back of the Indies, had reached Spanish shores unseized and undiminished. Meanwhile, Britain ached for the loss of her sailors, their lives spent for nothing "as the eccentricities of British Foreign Policy and their own wandering natures had directed them," their corpses "picked white by fishes as the tides rolled them among the treetops of a submarine forest," so Evelyn Waugh puts it in his *Vile Bodies*. In any case, it had been "a horrible experience that made a deep and lasting impression on the nation."

More impressed than most by the horrors of the Porto Bello disaster was an irascible half-pay naval officer with several years of experience in the West Indies, where he had seen action during the 1718–1720 war against Spain. This conflict had taught him to hold the Spanish navy in contempt—it had on every occasion refused to fight, remaining in sheltered harbors, or running at the sight of a British sail. He also knew from hard experience that Spain's greatest ally in the Caribbean was time and disease. Porto Bello, he asserted, should have been quickly taken, and could have been, with far fewer ships than had been present under Hosier's command.

But he was no longer a naval officer; he had become a politician and was now an MP representing the borough of Penryn, Cornwall. In this capacity he gave many fiery speeches in Parliament, advocating what was then called a "Blue Water" policy: In short, a strong navy would ensure domestic liberty by negating the need for a standing army that could, in the hands of a despot, be used to oppress the people. That navy would also protect British maritime trade abroad and act as a counterweight against the despotic land-based powers of Europe. And while a Whig, this ex-naval officer was a "Patriot," or "Country Whig," that is among those Whigs in opposition to Walpole, who believed his ministry corrupt, interested only in profit and at odds with Britain's best interests and national honor.

The name of this semiretired officer was Edward Vernon. His time would come. Meanwhile, the nation could only lament her losses, best expressed in Glover's ballad, later published and illustrated with the image of a destroyed ship and a crew of accusing, skeletal sailors, Admiral Hosier chief among them:

Heed, oh heed my fatal story,
I am Hosier's injured ghost:

You who now have purchased glory
At this place I was lost . . .
Think on revenge for my ruin,
And for England shamed in me.

8.

Soissons, an obscure, attractive city in the département de l'Aisne, in the green heart of France about sixty miles northeast of Paris, has found itself at the crossroads of world events several times in its 2,500 year history.

In 57 B.C.E., Caesar led his ironshod legions to the foot of its defensive palisades; the Suessiones, the Celtic tribe inhabiting the area, promptly surrendered their capital, thus beginning a long French military tradition. In 300 C.E., Soissons became one of the first Christian dioceses in Northern France, and acquired the "shoes of the virgin," a precious holy relic soon housed in the Abbey of Notre Dame, founded by France's pious Merovingian kings. Hopscotching across the centuries to the Hundred Years' War, in 1327 the city became the site of the notorious "Massacre of the English Archers," during which far more than the archers were killed: the King of France's army, breaching Soissons's walls after a lengthy siege, ran amuck, pillaging, raping and killing indiscriminately. French soldiers massacring the English was to be expected; French soldiers massacring other Frenchmen shocked France and the rest of Europe. Shakespeare references this lamentable event in *Henry V*: the king's famous speech "Once more unto the breach, dear friends . . ." was delivered to the English troops at the Battle of Agincourt, purposely fought on St. Crispin's Day, October 25, 1415—Saints Crispin and Crispianus being Soissons's patron saints.

More than three centuries later, in June 1728, representatives of Britain and Spain met in the Palace of the Counts of Soissons to resolve the inconclusive Anglo-Spanish War then still raging. They had already tried, unsuccessfully, in March of that year, at the El Pardo Palace in Madrid. That time, after some hard bargaining, the British Ambassador to Spain, Sir Benjamin Keene, and representatives of Spain's King Felipe, had arrived at terms later considered too lenient. These terms were repudiated by Walpole's ministry. Hence, this second attempt, eight months later, in a series of lengthy diplomatic meetings that became known as the Congress of Soissons.

Now on the British side we find a duo of sharpers—diplomat Sir Stephen Poyntz and Robert Walpole's younger brother, Horatio. Negotiations continued for another year, this as Hosier's fleet languished in the poisonous waters off Porto Bello, its British sailors dying by the dozens each day.

First, Horatio Walpole sought to impede the Spanish-Austrian alliance, already solidified in the Treaty of Vienna. In this, he was not successful. Then, he sought to confirm Spain's recognition of British possession of Gibraltar and Menorca; this he achieved at the price of acknowledging Spanish territorial rights in Sicily and Parma—Queen Isabela's cherished ambition for her sons. Trade issues, however, proved intractable. Britain wanted fewer restrictions on trade with Spanish colonies in the Americas and an end to the search and seizure of British merchant ships in West Indian waters by *guarda costa*. These seizures had already led to claims and counter claims sufficient to perplex both governments. But Spain held firm to the terms agreed upon in the Treaty of Utrecht. Of course, underlying Spanish obstinacy lay the vast amounts of contraband goods, carried by English ships and flooding their American colonies.

Horatio Walpole chose to pretend the extensive, organized smuggling now carried on by the South Sea Company and numerous private traders didn't exist. Spain knew better, having been briefed by two English traitors, whose testimony survives in the Spanish archives at Simancas.

"The Spanish archives are naturally richer in materials for the study of contraband trade than are the English repositories," wrote the distinguished Canadian historian Vera Lee Brown in 1924:

> While the English government wished to remain in official ignorance of the contraband activities of its subjects, the Spanish government was willing to pay well for circumstantial information which they realized would strengthen their position. . . . Much of the material is from English sources, the English company having been particularly unfortunate in faithless servants.

The "faithless servants" in question were two turncoat employees of the South Sea Company who, independent of each other, betrayed their country and sold themselves into the service of Spain: Dr. John Burnet and Matthew Plowes. Burnet, a South Sea Company factor at Cartagena had been financially ruined by Spanish seizures of Company property during the 1718–1720 war, and needed money. Plowes, highly placed in the Company— he was its recording secretary and chief accountant—may have had more complex reasons for betrayal, but money was also undoubtedly a prime motivator.

Negotiations at Soissons, seemingly endless, wound on through the winter of 1728 and into the following year. Spanish negotiators presented their list of grievances concerning British smuggling and violations of trade restrictions; the British pressed their claims regarding unjustly seized trading vessels, imprisoned sailors and lost merchandise. Overeager *guarda costa* captains, from the British point of view little better than pirates, seemed to be pushing the two countries toward yet another inconclusive war.

In August of 1729, in the middle of this mess, in the middle of the night, the chief Spanish negotiator at Soissons, the Marquis de Barrenechea, awoke to an insistent knocking at his door. It was Secretary Plowes, wearing a suitably rococo disguise and wrapped in a voluminous cloak, bearing a cache of forty-two documents stolen from South Sea Company vaults which would do great damage to his country's cause. The astonished marquis examined this trove as Plowes explained himself: his price for this information was £60 immediately, Plowes said, followed by asylum in Spain and a state pension of 500 doblones per year for life.

9.

The stolen documents fell into two general categories: the first described in detail the various subterfuges whereby the South Sea Company concealed contraband cargo in their vessels; the second provided lists of corrupt Spanish colonial officials who had been bribed to look the other way as the Company pursued its illicit activities. These officials included, astonishingly, the Viceroy of Mexico, who along with regular cash payments, had received "a sword garnished with diamonds and a very exquisite musical clock." The supercargo of the *Royal George*—the same ship that had been stranded in Porto Bello harbor at the beginning of Hosier's blockade—had paid out 118,000 pesos in bribes to the governor of that town to secure the release of his ship without the requisite examination of cargo called for by Spanish regulations.

Corruption ran very deep on the Spanish side. In one of Plowes's documents, a South Sea Company factor complained to his superiors, illustrating the typical sort of bribes necessary to do business in the Spanish Americas:

It is with great concern that we are obliged to tell Your Honours that we have been compelled by threats and menaces of having the intervention put upon us, to regale the Governor of Panama with 6000 *pesos de ocho*, the fiscal with 1500 and the two other Royal Officials with 1000 each and as Your Honours never sent a present to the General we were forced to purchase a ring for him with 2400 *pesos de ocho*, the same demands Your Honours must always expect from the Governor and royal officials.

Another choice document described secret contracts between Don Francisco de Alcibar, a prominent Spanish official in Buenos Aires, and Jesuit missionaries, then in the midst of their ill-fated civilizing mission to the Indians of Paraguay—all of whom were engaged in the illegal export of silver in exchange for British manufactured goods. Two Jesuit fathers made the trip to England aboard a South Sea Company vessel with over 400,000 pesos in silver concealed in their baggage.

But, perhaps the most damaging document of all implicated the Spanish representative to the South Sea Company in London charged with enforcing the regulations of the *Asiento*. This person can be counted among the greatest double agents of the eighteenth-century. Among his corrupt practices, the consistent undercounting of allowable trade cargo in the annual permission ships, which had cost the Spanish government thousands in lost revenue.

The Marquis de Barrenechea's eyes must have bugged out as he read over the stolen documents brought in by Plowes and similar material provided later by Dr. Burnet. The marquis judged them so important to ongoing negotiations at Soissons that he eschewed the usual practice of having all diplomatic material transcribed into French (then the lingua franca of diplomacy) and sent them on to the ministry in Madrid in the original English, endorsed and stamped by Plowes and Burnet and another turncoat, a South Sea Company ship's captain named Opie. They were later deposited in the Spanish Archives at Simancas. This is where Vera Lee Brown found them in the 1920s and became the first to read their bald account of corruption and diplomatic intrigue in two hundred years.

10.

Until Brown's discovery, the intractable position of Spanish negotiators at Soissions in 1728–29 seemed yet another example of Latin obstinacy in the face of a superior British bargaining position. Further digging in the archives turned up an accompanying report, authored by Dr. Burnet, that explored the depths of British smuggling activities and the consequent corruption of Spanish officials and offered a stern condemnation of the trade practices of the South Sea Company condoned, however tacitly, by the British Government: no ship sailing from England to the West Indies since 1715, Burnet charged, had failed to carry contraband—this included Royal Navy warships and every one of the slavers delivering the *piezas de Indias* under the *Asiento* Contract. South Sea Company ships in particular were riddled with secret compartments concealing manufactured goods, a far more lucrative trade than the transportation of slaves.

Burnet also explored the South Sea Company's practice of allowing its individual servants to engage in private side-deals, turning every factor, no matter now insignificant, into a smuggler.

"In this fashion," Brown asserts, "the Spanish American dominions were kept awash in illicit goods and legitimate traffic by the Spanish galleons suffered heavily."

The list of stolen documents still extant at Simancas also includes a copy of the English code cipher used by diplomatic representatives in communications with the Foreign Office; a variety of shipping invoices listing contraband goods going back to 1715; and even a copy of the secret instructions recently issued by the Spanish government to its own delegation at Soissons. This last document had been acquired for a stiff price from a corrupt naval officer at Madrid.

"Taken as a whole," comments Brown, "the documents secured from the South Sea Company secretary constituted as rich an assemblage of facts damaging to that organization as could well have been gathered from any quarter."

The impact of this trove on the negotiations at Soissons and their role in contributing to the war of 1739–1742, later named after the unfortunate Jenkins and his severed ear, cannot be overestimated. They immediately stiffened Spanish opposition to Horatio Walpole and the other English negotiators. As talks continued, the Marquis de Barrenechea smothered his rage at British duplicity under an exterior of aristocratic calm. But he refused to bend on the most contentious matter under discussion: the search and seizure of British ships in West Indian waters. He now knew with certainty they nearly all carried contraband goods. The South Sea Company had been cheating since the beginning, with the connivance of their government.

One of the documents, signed by the second mate of the *Royal George*, detailed a complex smuggling operation that occurred even as the delegates sat at Soissons:

The *Royal George*, while anchored at Porto Bello just before Hosier's blockade, had taken on an illegal treasure amounting to 386 chests and fifty-five cases of Spanish silver. Upon the vessel's release—after pressure from Hosier and the judicious application of substantial bribes—the ship was met by a sloop containing an additional 136 chests, two cases and one cask of silver. All this was speedily transferred to the *Royal George*'s hold. The presence of such riches in a single company ship might have raised eyebrows in England; rumors would certainly have reached the ears of the Spanish ambassador. South Sea Company officials hatched a plan to avoid this scrutiny: The *Royal George* sailed to the British island of Antigua and was there falsely condemned as unseaworthy. Crews then shifted its treasure to a waiting Royal Navy warship which sailed for England, transforming itself briefly into a smuggling vessel.

Spain had been a dupe, her honor insulted. The stolen documents illustrated her humiliation. At Soissons her representatives suddenly became truculent and unwilling to compromise. British negotiators began to suspect that Spain had somehow acquired secret information—though they didn't know its source. In the meantime, Plowes and Burnet continued to operate as double agents, feeding information to Spain. Because of them, the negotiations at Soissons ended in an inconclusive fizzle.

The tepid agreement called the Treaty of Seville that resulted, signed by the delegates on November 9, 1729, returned international matters to the status quo pre-1727, which is to say it reconfirmed the unworkable situation laid out in the Treaty of Utrecht. In the end, nothing got resolved. An outcome that can be laid directly at the feet of the two spies who sold out their country for cash.

So what happened to these two "faithless servants?" It is a sad truism that traitors generally finish well. Both Burnet and Plowes escaped judgement and hanging, though in Plowes case, just barely: information only he could have provided accusing the directors of the South Sea Company of vast frauds, used injudiciously in a letter published by the Spanish ambassador in the London press, clearly implicated the corrupt accountant. Plowes was in Soissons at the time; the directors ordered him home for questioning. Plowes panicked and threw himself at the mercy of the Marquis de Barrenechea. Thinking fast, the marquis arranged for Plowes to see a physician who then confirmed that an emergency surgery was necessary and that Plowes could not possibly travel. His medical condition was so grave, in fact, that he might be obliged to resign his post with the Company and retire to private life.

Around this time Dr. Burnet received a letter from a friend in London, reminding him of his duty to the Company and to the king. Clearly, he was also under suspicion. And yet neither Plowes nor Burnet lost their positions of trust. Plowes value to Spain, initially greater than Burnet's, faded out after the Congress disbanded. Two years later, we find him in Paris, unemployed and friendless "without the resources to supply the needs of himself and numerous family."

A final piece of correspondence in the Simancas archives shows him begging the Spanish government to make good on the pension they had promised him. They probably did; but no further records of the matter has been found and Plowes voice echoes no more. He disappears from history, a traitorous drop in the ocean of the past.

11.

Burnet, however, continued to be of service to Spain and seems to have been made from sterner stuff than Plowes. He wrote a damning and detailed report for his handlers. Burnet's nongrammatical Spanish necessitated the intervention of a Spanish official, a certain Don Andre de Otamendri who transcribed and organized the material. This report must have become required reading for all Spanish government officials serving in the American colonies. Divided into six detailed sections, it can still be found in the Simancas archives.

Section 1, *Sobre Commercio Ilicito*, describes every trick the British employed in secreting contraband goods aboard their vessels: the hidden compartments built into ships meant to carry African slaves; the false bills of lading; the fast local sloops adding to the legitimate cargos of the permission ships at a prearranged rendezvous, some isolated lagoon or desert island; the unmarked cargo loaded and unloaded in the dead of night; such operations, Burnet adds, usually supervised by Jews in the Company's employ, who knew "very well how to handle goods at our wharfs in the night time without any notice being taken of them."

In one memorable instance, sailors aboard an English ship supposed to be carrying *piezas de Indias* for the market at Cartagena, but in fact carrying manufactured goods, were ordered by their captain to paint themselves up in blackface and pose as slaves exercising on deck—an absurd camouflage to deter passing *guarda costa* cutters. That this ploy apparently worked stands as an indictment of the nautical telescopes of the day.

In much of the smuggling activities, Burnet continues, the Royal Navy was deeply involved—as seen with the *Royal George* incident. The navy provided protection for Company ships from both *guarda costa* privateers and pirates of the more conventional sort, with navy captains receiving a percentage of the profits of smuggling runs. Less than half the silver exported from the Spanish colonies left the West Indies legally, Burnet says. Contraband trade was ruining the Spanish colonial economy; dealers in such goods, immune to all customs duties, undercut legitimate merchants at the trade fairs of Porto Bello and Cartagena by fifty percent or more.

To support his incendiary charges, Burnet enlisted his wife. He had most recently been the South Sea Company's factor at Cartagena. His wife had remained there during his sojourn at Soissons. Now he sent her special instructions: she was to pack up all his personal papers, company documents, bills of lading, and other documents and ship them to him in Madrid, where he had gone to consult with his new masters. She did as he asked—and took ship with the chests of pilfered documents to join him. With this new information in hand, Burnet concluded his damning report, its penultimate section *De Contravenciones* offering a fatal prescription to end contraband trade that would lead directly to war in 1739. He called for the maintenance of "an adequate number of *guarda costas* capable of seizing whatever foreign vessel might appear on the coast."

The Spanish government took this draconian recommendation to heart—though they ignored his more reasonable suggestion that to truly end smuggling "a frequent and abundant supply of goods from Spain . . . should reach American shores." But totalitarian governments, then as now, will choose enforcement (more prisons! more police!) over amelioration in most circumstances.

In the decade following 1729, Spanish *guarda costa* seizures of British merchant vessels increased in number and viciousness. The incarceration and mistreatment of British crews also increased along with official encouragement of vicious semipiratical *guarda costa* captains like Juan de León Fandiño, villain of the attack on the *Rebecca* and Captain Jenkins in 1731. The violated Welshman's severed ear stands as a vivid symbol for what had become, by 1738, a "Depredations Crisis" for British merchants dealing in the West Indies.

The British government wanted a free exchange of British goods for Spanish silver; the rigid mercantile system adhered to by Spain did not allow for such an exchange—even though they could not supply their own colonies with those goods needed to maintain a decent standard of living. But the inhabitants of the Spanish Colonies were, in the end, the arbiter of world events: smuggling will always exist where there also exists an appetite for what is smuggled—viz the "War on Drugs" of our own era.

As payment for betraying his country, Burnet asked he be made an inspector general of the Caracas Company, a Spanish trading concern modeled on the South Sea. This request was denied. He'd betrayed his own people in a similar position, why would he not do so again for the right inducements? Desperate and short of funds he then asked that he be appointed *médico de cámara* to the Spanish Navy. He was a doctor, after all, a graduate of the University of Edinburgh, and had been a medical adviser to Hosier's doomed fleet. He also asked for an officer's appointment for his nephew.

Despite Hosier's fate and the horrific deathrate on Royal Navy ships in 1727–29, both these requests were granted.

Like Plowes, Burnet then vanishes from the official record. No one knows where their bones lie or their ultimate fates, beyond that which awaits all men. Then end results of their treachery, however, would have shattering consequences—and result in the war after which Captain Jenkins's excised auricular appendage is perhaps unfairly named.

12.

July 1737 finds the melancholic Spanish King Felipe V once again abed in his palace in Madrid. Wallowing in his own filth, clinging to his wife's tattered nightgown, visited alternately with vivid night terrors and deep, days-long lethargies. He refused to shave or bathe and would only eat a few spoonfuls of tepid soup daily and only if served by his wife's own hand. This had been going on for half a year. The affairs of Spain, both domestic and international, had suffered from his incapacitation. Even his wife, Queen Isabela, de facto ruler of the Spanish Empire, could not quite do without him. When clean and sober and temporarily dispossessed of his madness, he showed a shrewd grasp of state matters as befits a nephew of the great Louis XIV.

And there was something more: In the hierarchical, deeply conservative Spain of the Grandees, the king, mad or not, sat at the top like God in Heaven. All power emanated from the throne. Lying in bed, nearly catatonic, he was useless to his country and his queen. Something had to done. The power of her sexual blandishments had faded with age; though the king, even semitorpid as he was, still sought his release with unusual frequency in the sanctioned joys of marital embrace, sex failed to rouse him as before.

The court physician, Dr. Giuseppe Cervi, a man ahead of his time, recommended music therapy as a cure for melancholia in general, and he now prescribed it for Felipe. But to cure a king would take a very great musician indeed. Only one, Cervi believed, might be equal to such a task, the great Italian *castrato* opera singer, Farinelli, who was just then in Paris on a European tour and would soon be coming to Madrid. After a recent performance at Versailles, King Louis XV had presented the castrated wonder with a golden snuff-box emblazoned with the royal portrait surrounded by diamonds.

Carlo Maria Michelangelo Nicola Broschi—stage name Farinelli—born near Naples in 1705, is the most famous representative of a bizarre tradition in Italian sacred music, going back centuries. Choirboys, caught before their voices changed, were shorn of their testicles. This act of mutilation preserved the vocal range initially shared by both sexes before it succumbs to the corrosive effects of testosterone. Castratos maintained a prepubescent flexibility of voice, combined with the lung power of a mature male, and were much sought after by opera directors, when that genre became popular in the seventeenth-century. According to contemporary listeners the effects were otherworldly, like listening to the angels, themselves unsexed, sing in heaven.

Farinelli's fanatical admirers in England, where he performed under contract for a company called the Opera of the Nobility, were mostly aristocratic and female; they swooned over his performances and showered him with cash and expensive gifts. He had just completed two triumphant seasons there. With Farinelli mania at its peak, one enthusiastic patron, said to be a certain Lady Rich, loudly declared from her box at the opera during a Farinelli performance "One God! One Farinelli!" The audience gasped, but this blasphemous phrase became a sort of eighteenth-century meme, depicted on snuff boxes, and mocked in the satirical prints of Hogarth. Farinelli was the rock star of his day, complete with groupies and sycophants—albeit one lacking the ability to shag them Mick Jagger-style.

The physical side effects of castration at an early age are both debilitating and strange. The absence of testosterone keeps bone joints pliable; oddly long limbs and a massive rib-cage results, giving castrati a gawky, alien look. Pulmonary development allowed them to maintain notes as high as C6, the top of the range, for literally breathtaking lengths of time. Composers treasured this ability; operas were composed specifically with castrati in mind. The practice of mutilating boys for musical effect mercifully ceased in the mid-nineteenth century. A creaky recording exists of the last castrato, Alessandro Moreschi, taken in 1902 at the Vatican; the poor fellow was by then middle-aged and no longer at the peak of his powers but the sound he produces is entrancingly strange, neither male nor female; the voice of an androgynous, aging cherubim.

Italian authorities exhumed what remained of Farinelli's bones from a cemetery in Bologna in 2006 and subjected them to a pitiless examination. The soil was acidic, the bones in poor condition, but the odd elongation of limb and insect-like jaw could still be discerned. A few critical accounts in the eighteenth-century London press describe Farinelli's absurd, awkward presence on the stage: he barely moved, they complained, he could sing but dramatic skills eluded him completely. A contemporary sketch shows him in a dress, playing a woman's part, looking like a cross between a praying mantis and a marionette, invisible strings moving his flexible joints from the rafters. Nonetheless, Queen Isabela now pinned all her hopes on the great castrato.

On August 25, 1737, just a few days after Farinelli had begun the Spanish leg of his European tour, Queen Isabela brought him to the antechamber just outside the king's bedroom. There, the castrato sang five or six Italian arias, his personal favorites. This performance repeated over several nights managed to rouse the king from his mental slumber. At last, Felipe emerged, bleary-eyed, bearded, and stinking, as usual, wearing his wife's cast-off night-gown. He praised Farinelli's wonderful singing and, per tradition, granted any reward the castrato might ask as compensation for his performance. Later in life Farinelli told the English musicologist Charles Burney that he had been coached by Queen Isabelala to ask the king, as a special favor, to bathe, shave, dress, and join the Queen for dinner.

This request, Felipe reluctantly granted. Over the next few days he once again took his place as the King of Spain—though the cure remained incomplete and constantly in need of renewal. Felipe insisted that Farinelli accept a position in the royal house-hold as *musico de camera* and *familiar criado*, which is to say the king's personal musician. Farinelli had no choice but to acquiesce, became indispensable to the royal household, and never again sang in public. But with these appointments he and his family rose in society; extravagant gifts and estates were showered upon him. Aristocratic antecedents somehow discovered in the Broschi family tree, Farinelli was made a Spanish knight and his scheming brother Riccardo eventually became Spain's Minister of War.

Meanwhile, the castrato sang for King Felipe every evening at dinner, always the same four or five songs sung that first night. Though, as the British ambassador Sir Benjamin Keene remarked, these performances had unintended side effects. In a letter to the Duke of Newcastle, Keene describes the surreal scene at the royal table:

> Your grace must smile when I inform you that the King himself imitates Farinelli some times air after air, and some-times after the musick is over, and throws himself into such Freaks and howlings, that all possible means are taken to prevent people from being witness to his Follies.

There was, however, a more serious consequence to Farinelli's command position at the Spanish court. He had been effectively removed from his adoring London public, his ironclad contract with the Opera of Nobility broken. Given the sensitive Anglo-Spanish situation and the escalating seizures of English merchant ships by *guarda costas* in the West Indies, Farinelli's "detention" by Spain took on vivid political overtones. Farinelli, the London papers said, had been stolen in the same way their ships were "detained in the Caribbean by the Spanish Guard Coasts." Here was yet another example of illegal Spanish appropriation of British property.

The directors of the Opera of Nobility naturally objected to the "theft" of Farinelli, which to them would mean an entire season's revenue lost, not to mention production costs already invested, and thus, probable bankruptcy. In an open letter to King Felipe, the directors "unanimously resolved" that they could not release Farinelli from his contract, "considering the great loss, they must sustain by his absence, all the Operas being performed this season, so far advanced that it is absolutely impossible to supply his place."

But their protests, at once angry and impotent, failed to influence the Spanish king who refused a single peso of compensation for his appropriation of their star.

The castrato would stay in Madrid for the rest of his professional life—though his performances were now limited to King Felipe, his wife, and a few hardy courtiers. Farinelli eventually retired to Bologna where he died in 1782, Carlo Broschi again, lonely and embittered, having out-lasted all his friends and admirers, reliving in memory the years when he had been worshipped as a god by opera lovers, one of the first pan-European celebrities.

13.

The appropriation of Farinelli by Spain became the talk of London in 1737–38 and the source of much indignation. A conversation overheard by Sir Thomas Geraldino—an Irishman in the Spanish service, then Spanish ambassador to London—characterizes the English attitude: "That the King of Spain did not let Farinello return; and that it is Farinello who wants to remain because of the 3,500 Doblones—" though his compensation has been reported at considerably more than this, up to £14,000 per year, including a mule drawn coach, gold, diamonds and other blandishments.

Spain, her king, and Farinelli herself were denounced in mock-heroic style articles and letters in the London press. Walpole himself was blamed, the opera singer's defection to the Spanish court seen as a living symbol of Spanish attacks on British shipping in the Caribbean.

"The coincidence of Farinelli's detention in Spain with the increasing captures of British shipping was too obvious to miss," writes musical historian Thomas McGeary. "Journalists and satirists of the opposition quickly put the Farinelli affair to political ends. The opposition periodicals . . . regularly returned to [it] to score political points at Walpole's expense. . . . Images of London enchanted and enraptured by Farinelli's singing symbolized a lethargic and enervated Britain under Walpole's pacific policy of submitting to Spanish depredations; and the Spanish court's 'detention' of Farinelli and breach of the opera director's contract was a convenient parallel to Spain's capturing British merchant ships, violating treaties and depriving the South Sea Company of its commercial rights."

The anti-Walpole journal *Common Sense*, writing of Farinelli's defection to Spain, reported that "several pretty Gentlemen and Ladies, whom the Depredations in America never in the least affected were Thunder-struck at the fatal Report, and were no sooner recovered from their Surprize, but several indecent Expressions were thrown out against his Spanish Majesty for this unheard of Outrage. . . . Cries a Lady of exquisite Taste 'What are the taking of a few Ships, and the cutting off the Ears of the Masters of our Merchantmen, to the loss of our dear, dear Farinello?'"

The anonymous author of this piece kept both feet firmly planted in the waters of sarcasm, after the fashion of the times, but behind the satirical tone loomed an international imbroglio the "Depredations Crisis" which would at last, inevitably, lead to the wider war everyone dreaded.

14.

One imagines Captain Robert Jenkins knocking around London coffeehouses and Bristol sailors' taverns and the seas of the world for seven more years with his ear "preserved in a bottle" or some say in a small box swathed in cotton wool. For the price of a pint or a tot of rum he displays this grisly artifact and tells his oft-repeated tale of Spanish barbarity on the high seas, the same story he had once told to the king himself. When would justice be done?

True, the famous ear, removed by the brutal *guarda costa* captain Fandiño, had initially inspired a flurry of sternly worded diplomatic correspondence. But by 1737, the "ear matter" had receded into the past, forgotten as other more recent and more outrageous incidents came to replace it in the public imagination: Captain Thomas Weir, "Maimed of Both Arms," bedbound murdered along with eight of his crew by Spanish officials; Captain King of the *Runslet*, tortured with gunlock screws and lighted matches. . . .

In the intervening years, Jenkins went back to sea on the West Indies route and later for the East India Company, haunting his own life like a ghost missing an ear. Justice had eluded him along with any sort of compensation for his stolen property or battered and mutilated body. Walpole's ministry, committed to peace above all, sought to downplay Spanish atrocities. Walpole himself still believed firmly that a government interested in making money could negotiate or buy itself out of any crisis. His attitude might be described as affably corrupt or perhaps inadvertently humanitarian; war's ultimate cost in British lives and treasure would always outweigh any injury to national honor, the sacrifice of a few ships and cargos, the imprisonment of a few dozen sailors, the severing of an ear. These things were just the cost of doing business.

Meanwhile, British losses in the West Indies mounted. Spanish *guarda costas* had grown increasingly aggressive. The presence of a single Spanish piece of eight, standard currency throughout the Caribbean, found aboard an English ship was enough to condemn it as a smuggler, with its cargo seized and its crew imprisoned in the dungeons of Havana's Morro Castle. At last the growing political opposition to Walpole in Parliament took up the debate regarding Spanish depredations with a new intensity: Spain must be made to pay damages or war would result.

A petition seeking "to procure speedy and ample satisfaction for the Losses . . . sustained and that no British vessel be detained or searched on the High Seas" sent to King George in October 1737 bore the signatures of 149 prominent merchants. To this document they had affixed a list of ships ransacked or seized by *guarda costas* in the West Indies. This list went back several years and was accompanied by details regarding each incident. Toward the bottom could be found the case of the *Rebecca*, Captain Jenkins, and his severed ear.

Unusually, upon receiving this petition, the ministry acted quickly. The king himself had taken an interest; perhaps he remembered that poor fellow Jenkins whose ear had been cut off, and who had petitioned him personally for redress back in '31 and never got any. The merchants' new petition was then examined by a Special Committee of the King's Privy Council:

"His Majesty was so sensibly touched with the losses and sufferings of His Trading Subjects," Secretary Newcastle commented, "that he was pleased immediately to direct a Memorial to be prepared."

The resulting "memorial"—or diplomatic memorandum—more sternly worded than usual, forwarded to the Spanish court via Ambassador Keene in Madrid, kicked off a new round of intense negotiations. Both nations, apparently, hoped to avoid another war. But this was also an era of nostalgia for a glorious past inimical to such negotiations: Spain hankered for the deeds of the Conquistadors; England for Drake and Sir Walter Raleigh and the Great Elizabeth.

The Spanish government had now fallen into the hands of a quartet of hard-liners: Ustaritz, first commissioner of the War Office; Commercial Minister De la Quadra; Marine Secretary Quintana; and Montijo, president of the Council of the Indies, all united under the authority of Queen Isabela, the king too busy howling at dinner to Farinelli's tunes to pay much attention to the affairs of his country. Within the Queen's often mercurial and whimsical oversight, this Gang of Four ruled Spain. "The country is at present governed by three or four mean, stubborn people of little minds and limited understandings," Keene complained from Madrid, "but full of the Romantick Ideas they have found in old Memorials and Speculative authors who have treated of the immense Grandeur of the Spanish Monarchy, People who have vanity enough to think of themselves reserved by Providence to rectify and reform the mistakes and abuses of past ministers and ages."

The Spanish Gang of Four at first tried to reject British claims. Many of the claims had passed their expiration date, their details vague, documentation and ship's manifests lost. Jenkins's and *Rebecca* fell into this category. But Parliamentary pressure on Walpole to do something became impossible to ignore. The multitude of older claims, unresolved and nearly forgotten, merely underscored the opposition's point: that only long delays and oblivion could be expected from Spanish justice. The merchant's petition of October now inspired a series of increasingly urgent diplomatic memorandums all sent to the Spanish ministry through Keene. Each detailed more unresolved claims. The harried ambassador presented an additional twenty-eight bundles of claims and depositions. The Gang of Four regarded this welter of paperwork with disdain. Keene reported Montijo's words on the matter to Secretary Newcastle:

"If Spain would accumulate her grievances," Montijo said, according to Keene, "she might make as much to do as England did . . . that there were Faults on Both Sides; England's contrabandists ought to be punished as well as some of the Spanish Governors Hanged."

Still, Montijo, generally regarded as the most conciliatory of the four, was willing to negotiate. Meanwhile, the mood in England, hardening, edged toward war, with the London press and the pamphleteers, all members of that "malicious tribe of writers," beating the drums. Now an ocean of verbiage poured from the pens of Grub Street—plays, ballads, masques, satires, articles, editorials—all advocating war with Spain. The anti-Walpolean journal *The Craftsman* led the opposition press in its vehemence and powers of invention: it accused Wapole of failing to protect English trade from "Pyratical Depredations and cruel treatment of our Seamen," and reported a particularly incendiary story that was at best half-true. English sailors "enslaved" in Havana, *The Craftsman* said, were forced to work on labor gangs in chains, "ragged, meager, and half-starved."

"Are our brave English Mariners to be thus abused, who have committed no Crime, and whom the Spaniards durst not look in the face upon equal Terms, were their Hands unty'd?" went a typical *Craftsman* editorial.

The sailors in question comprised the crew of two ships, the *Loyal Charles* and *Dispatch*, both of London. These vessels were well known to the merchants of that city; the imprisoned sailors in effect, native sons. The opposition press got busy pleading the sailor's cause. Popular prints—the political cartoons of the day—showed them skeletal and beaten, laboring under the Spanish lash. But this was mostly eighteenth-century "fake news." The British Consul at Cádiz, appointed to look into the matter, eventually found the sailors under house arrest in that city, not laboring in chains, being fed, given clothes and shelter, and treated reasonably well. This intelligence was largely ignored. The image of free Englishmen tortured and enslaved at the hands of cruel Spanish papists could not be dislodged from the popular imagination.

15.

More vicious parliamentary debates followed. Merchants and sea captains who had been brutalized by *guarda costas* in the West Indies were asked to testify before a special committee of the House.

Historians agree that Captain Jenkins, his case singled out, perhaps for its picturesque qualities (what's not to like about a severed ear?) was among those called to tell his tale of woe. The *House of Commons Journal*, official record of the doings of the legislature, listed the following item on March 16, 1738: "Ordered, that Captain Robert Jenkins do attend this House immediately." Apparently, Jenkins didn't show. The next day came a second summons: "Ordered that Captain Robert Jenkins do attend on Tuesday morning next, the Committee of the Whole house to whom the Petition of divers merchants interested in the British plantations in America and many others is referred." Similar orders, though Jenkins is not mentioned specifically, followed on March 21, 22, 23, and 30.

Did Jenkins appear or not? Here's where things get tricky. Unfortunately, transcripts of House testimony from this period have not survived; controversy over this point still rages. In fact, nothing certain is known of Jenkins's movements between 1738 and 1741 when he was appointed temporary governor of the island of St. Helena, then an East India Company refueling station in the South Atlantic. Some historians, crediting contemporary press accounts, assert that Jenkins answered the summons and made a dramatic, epoch-making presentation before the House, brandishing the blackened remnants of his ear:

"Jenkins was examined before a committee of the House of Commons," says the account in the Dictionary of National Biography, (DNB):

> His story lost nothing in the telling; he produced something which he asserted was the ear that had been cut or torn off, and being asked "what were his feelings when he found himself in the hands of such barbarians," he replied (in what became a famous phrase), "I committed my soul to God and my cause to my country." The report roused the utmost public indignation.

Other historians insist that Jenkins never uttered this rousing response, that the patriotic sentiments ascribed to him, first reported in the *Gentleman's Magazine*, had been invented by MP William Pulteney, one of Walpole's most vocal and nimble-tongued parliamentary opponents. They generally place Jenkins out of England at the time of the debates, hence his failure to respond to the initial summons.

For roughly 150 years, historical consensus—which had come to see the war given Jenkins's name as wholly unnecessary and a national tragedy—doubted his story altogether. The man probably never existed! The tale of the severed ear was a fiction, or at least heavily embellished by opposition politicians seeking to destroy Walpole's successful and peaceable ministry. A few admitted the reality of Jenkins himself and even that his ear might had been severed but suggested the unfortunate mariner had lost it the pillory, to which he'd been condemned for various petty larcenies.

Archdeacon William Coxe, one of the earliest historians of the Walpolean era, writing in 1796, credited Jenkins's appearance before the House with great reluctance and looked with a jaundiced eye on the inciting ear-severing, which he called "this ridiculous story."

"According to contemporary accounts," Coxe wrote, emphasizing the element of hearsay, "[Jenkins] related the transaction with many additional circumstances of insult and barbarity, and displayed the ear, which he had preserved, as some assert in a box, and others in a bottle."

Coxe passed on his skepticism to historians of the next generation who came to regard the severing of Jenkins's ear as a complete myth, no more than anti-Walpolean propaganda, invented by the *Gentleman's Magazine* and repeated by other opposition journals. A peculiarity of press censorship of the times added greatly to the confusion: newspapers, prevented by law from printing House debates verbatim, resorted to a variety of creative subterfuges. The *London Magazine*, for example, reported on the speeches of a "learned and political club," in which prominent MPs were given Roman names—behind which the actual figures might be discerned lurking by contemporary readers, like Polonious behind the curtain in *Hamlet*. The euphemistic Senatorial debates of "Magna Lilliputa" featured in another publication.

The early twentieth-century historian William Thomas Laprade blamed such tactics for misconceptions, exaggerations and outright lies—often resorted to when "a publication was in a pinch" for news. Laprade numbered among those who considered the tale of Jenkins's eloquent testimony before the House as wholly untrue. Laprade believed that though summoned to testify, Jenkins never did, that he was "otherwise engaged and did not go." In the late 1940s, historian A. J. Henderson supported this view, asserting a new narrative he presented as "the truth":

"Jenkins was not in London, nor even in England at the time of the investigation (March 1738)" Henderson declared. "He was aboard his ship, the *Harrington*, homeward bound from a voyage to the West Indies; and he did not arrive in London until May 25, which was five days after Parliament had been prorogued for the summer."

However, against this debunking, it must be remembered that until the dogged researches of naval historian J. K. Laughton in 1898, the existence of Jenkins and his ear was utterly dismissed by nearly every reputable historians. These men were apparently not aware of—or had rejected—the early account published in Franklin's *Pennsylvania Gazette* in 1731. Laughton, during the course of an exhaustive investigation, discovered a cache of letters between Rear Admiral Charles Stewart, commander in chief at the Jamaica Station, his superiors, and several Spanish colonial officials. In his groundbreaking article published in the *English Historical Review,* Laughton wrote:

Whilst recently making some researches into the admiralty records, I came accidentally on a correspondence which seems to have hitherto escaped notice, which is interesting from the very clear light it throws on the state of our naval and mercantile relations in the West Indies for some years previous to the declaration of war with Spain in 1739. Incidentally also it confirms the story of Jenkins's ear, which for certainly more than a hundred years has been generally believed to be a fable.

Laughton then prints, for the first time, several of these records, silencing the ear-doubters for good.

In a letter from Laughton's trove, dated Oct. 12, 1731, Rear Admiral Charles Stewart first mentions Jenkins:

"I was a little surprised to hear of the usage Captain Jenkins met with off the Havana," he writes to Secretary of State Newcastle, "as I know the Governor there has the character of being an honest good man, and don't find anybody thinks he would connive or countenance such villainies."

To this letter Stewart appends a copy of his letter of protest, written in quite a different mood and sent to "his Excellency Dionisio Martinez de la Vega, Governor of Havana." This one reads in part:

> I have repeated assurances that you allow vessels to be fitted out of your harbor, particularly one Fandiño, and others who have committed the most cruel piratical outrages on several ships and vessels . . . particularly about the 20th April last sailed out of your harbour in one of those Guarda Costas, and met a ship of this island bound for England; and after using the captain in the most barbarous inhuman manner, taking all his money, cutting off one of his ears, plundering him of those necessaries which were to carry the ship safe home, without doubt with the intent that she should perish in the passage.

Laughton rescued Captain Jenkins and his ear from the realm of politically motivated fairy tale. Post-Laughton historians, now unable to deny that Jenkins lost his ear to Fandiño's cutlass, maintained instead that the incident really didn't matter that much. Philip Woodfine, writing in the 1980s, suggests that Jenkins's mutilation had no role in inciting the war that bears his name. The *Craftsman*'s account of the enslaved British sailors, Woodfine says, held more weight in parliamentary debates and with the public. By 1738, Woodfine concludes, "the episode of Jenkins' ear was an old one, not unique in its cruelty, not refreshed by any recent publication, and not supported by any appearance before the House."

And yet the wealth of surviving cultural evidence stands against this view. In the journals, newspapers, popular prints, and dramatic presentations of the years 1737–39, severed ears abound. They seem to appear just about everywhere. Allegorical dramatic pieces, often satirical in nature, portrayed Jenkins and his ear. One memorable masquerade performed in February 1739 featured, according to a contemporary account a "Spaniard, very richly dressed, who called himself knight of the Ear; as a Badge of which order, he wore on his Breast the form of a Star, whose Points seem'd ting'd with Blood, on which was painted an Ear, and round it, writtin in Capital letters, the word Jenkins."

Popular ballads sing of English merchants losing their ears; prints show an aggrieved Jenkins, ear in hand, trying to interest an indifferent government in his cause. (Cartoon-like and often brilliantly colored, political prints were collected with avidity by the average citizen in eighteenth-century England, as comic books were collected by most American kids in the 1950s and '60s.) One of the most popular prints of 1738 depicts a chaotic scene in Walpole's ministerial office:

There's the Great Man himself, the "Skreenmaster General," at his desk offering a "talk to the hand" gesture to a distraught Captain Jenkins displaying his piece of ear as a black servant removes the mariner's wig to show the healed-over stump. In the foreground a small dog tears up the *Asiento* contract and another minister obliviously pays court to a seated lady. In the background, a Walpolean flunky shows the door to a London merchant bearing a long list of English ships seized by *guarda costas*. No one in this scene pays any real attention to the injured and outraged Jenkins, symbol of Spanish cruelty and English national dishonor.

Also, there's just something about a severed ear. It has a kind of psychological power not easily dismissed, existing on a shadow line between the funny and the horrible. A severed ear sticks to the ribs of the imagination—think of Van Gogh's famous act of self-mutilation, or the bloody ear found in the grass in David Lynch's seriocomic *noir* thriller, *Blue Velvet*. And of course, there's the ear struck from the head of the High Priest's servant by the Apostle Peter in the New Testament: "Thus Simon Peter, who had a sword, drew it, struck the high priest's slave, and cut off his right ear. The slave's name was Malchus." (John 18:10) Here's Luke's version: "His disciples realized what was about to happen, and they asked, 'Lord shall we strike with a sword?' And one of them struck the high priest's servant and cut off his right ear. But Jesus said in reply, 'Stop, no more of this!' then he touched the servant's ear and healed him." (Luke 22:49–51)

Indeed the tale of Jenkins's severed ear made such an impression on the historian Carlyle that—in keeping with his famously arch literary style—he named the war after it and the name stuck, to the dismay of later, sober-sided modern historians like Woodfine.

16.

As public opinion called for war—fanned by the opposition press and by London theaters—complicated negotiations to avert it continued between Britain and Spain. Meanwhile, Walpole's ministry, recognizing its own precarious hold on a restive populace, shaded into tyranny: censorship became the order of the day. Walpole began to shut down the most vociferous opposition journals and those Drury Lane theatres where anti-government sentiment ran hottest. Walpole invoked the "Stage Licensing Act" passed by Parliament in 1737, a draconian piece of legislation that allowed for the suppression of theatrical pieces critical of government policy. With its usual sarcasm, *The Craftsman* made the point that such suppression of free expression was the chief attribute of tyranny. In a much read satirical piece they demanded certain passages decrying bad government in some of Shakespeare's famous plays be excised— and then quoted the passages verbatim, all of which might be easily applied to Walpole's regime.

Though *The Craftsman*, backed by powerful opposition politicians, could not be shut down outright, its print-jobber, a certain Henry Haines, was promptly arrested and thrown into jail. This unfortunate contractor was held without bail awaiting trial for two years.

Also, around this time, an actor named James Lacy produced an "oratory" (a kind of staged reading performed in a rented hall) on a historical subject that bore a strong resemblance to the Depredations Crisis. The plot of this oratory followed the true story of a fourteenth-century mayor of London and merchant named Philipot. In 1378, Philipot outfitted a private navy, recruited over one thousand sailors and went after a nest of Spanish pirates then preying on English shipping. Philipot's navy engaged the pirates in a pitched battle off the Spanish coast; fifteen pirate ships went to the bottom, thus putting an end to a threat the king and his ministers had failed to suppress. But upon returning to London a hero, the bold and enterprising Philipot was arrested for "waging war without official authorization." Public outcry eventually secured his release and a knighthood.

Parallels between Philipot's story and the political situation of 1738 could not have failed to strike the audiences of that year. The first performance of Lacy's Oratory was interrupted by constables. Nine actors ran; only Lacy held the boards to insist on his rights as an artist and a patriot to perform the piece. Arrested and "condemned without trial to Bridewell Prison for six months of hard labor," he was soon sprung by opposition politicians. But opposition assistance to Lacy and a few other actors did not preclude other forms of Walpolean oppression: an entire issue of *The Craftsman* supporting Lacy's cause disappeared. Confiscated and carried off in coaches, not a single example survived the censoring fires lit by authorities.

The press might be muzzled by actions such as these, but Walpole could not squelch the increasingly bellicose mood of the people, nor silence Hosier's ghost, crying out for vengeance. The country moved inexorably toward war—or as Temperley has it, by early 1738: "The atmosphere began to grow dark, the thunder to mutter and the storm seemed on the point of breaking."

17.

In Madrid, Ambassador Keene, who felt a genuine affection for the Spanish people, was determined to prevent the "storm from breaking." Unfortunately, the Spanish Gang of Four remained unmoved on the subject of compensation for seized English ships and abused crews. English West Indian merchants continued to demand swift action from Walpole's government; the opposition press continued to agitate on their behalf. At last, on March 2, 1738, Secretary of State Newcastle wrote to Keene with stunning news:

> His majesty has thought fit to declare that he will grant Letters of Reprisal to such of His Subjects whose Ships or effects may have been seized on the High Seas by Spanish garda costas or ships acting by Spanish Commissions, which is what His Majesty thinks he could not in Justice any longer Delay.

The letter of reprisal, an ancient tool, allowed hundreds of Philipots to muster their own navies. Aggrieved merchants were now urged to arm their vessels and turn themselves into privateers. That none did emphasizes the practical, not the piratical: the age of Philipot had long passed; without the support of a professional navy, such a move against another sovereign nation only invited disaster. It did, however, send a message to Spain. Two weeks after the granting of reprisals, on March 17, "the inimitable Captain Jenkins is believed to have presented to a sympathetic House of Commons his tale of woe together with his ear in a bottle." Two weeks after this semimythic appearance, on March 30, Captain Clinton, commander in chief of the Mediterranean Fleet received secret orders to take his ships from Gibraltar to Menorca and prepare for war. And in an even more provocative gesture, Commodore Charles Brown was sent to Jamaica with a squadron of ten war ships. His instructions: "to seize such armed vessels of Spain that cruised and lurked about under the notion of Garda Costas in order to take the ships and vessels of His Majesty's subjects."

The dispatching of Brown to the West Indies is seen by many as the true opening salvo in the as yet undeclared war.

Meanwhile, aided by Walpole's ministry, peace still threatened to break out. Ambassador Keene wrote to Newcastle on April 18, 1738: "I have omitted no occasion of setting this [Spanish] Court right in its notions about the Motives of the present general dissatisfaction in England, and of convincing them that it does not arise from any Intrigues of Party, but from the just resentment of the whole Nation occasioned by the cruel treatment His Majesty's subjects have received from the Spaniards."

Keene was an amiable fat man, a life-long bachelor, fond of fancy clothes and parties, and liked by many in Spain where he had lived for years; but beneath his pleasant rotundity, lurked a first-class diplomatic mind. He now made another vigorous appeal to la Quadra in Madrid: "As yet, the whole matter was *dans son entier* . . . absolutely in the hands of Spain to put a happy conclusion to it," he pleaded to the grandee.

To everyone's surprise, the usually haughty la Quadra relented. He was a proud man but not stupid. The letters of reprisal and Clinton's naval maneuvers had shaken him. He knew Spain, with its half-destroyed navy and nearly bankrupt treasury could ill afford another war. The payment of reparations perhaps offered a cheaper solution. At last la Quadra sent instructions to the Council of the Indies to draw up documents "in a manner to let them perceive that His Catholick Majesty's Intentions were to cultivate a good Understanding with the King of Great Britain and to render justice to such of his subjects as had been injured by the guarda costas." At the same time a separate set of instructions, sent to the Spanish colonial governors and other officials tasked with investigating British claims, ordered them to skew the numbers in favor of Spain.

Secretary of State Newcastle, forecasting just such Spanish foot-dragging, initiated more preparations for war. Another British squadron under the veteran Admiral Nicholas Haddock, consisting of nine ships and two fireships, was now dispatched to the Mediterranean with instructions to menace the Spanish coasts. Here was a vital instrument—perhaps the most efficient war-making machine in the world at that time—poised to fire a shot into the heart of Spain. By June 1738, war again seemed a moment away as parliamentary debates raged on:

"War is called for without Doors," cried Walpole apologist MP Henry Pelham, "it is called for within Doors; but Gentlemen don't consider how little you can gain by War."

"Let us exert the Courage that our Wrongs have inspired us with: In short, let us tread in the Steps of Former Ages," responded the silver-tongued Pulteney, conjuring the glories of the Elizabethan sea dogs, victors over the Spanish Armada in 1588.

South Sea Company factors in the Spanish ports now received covert warnings to evacuate with their families and merchandize. Meanwhile, the Admiralty issued orders for the press-ganging of sailors sufficient to crew a substantial naval force. (This brutal practice—essentially kidnapping legitimized by the government— persisted into the nineteenth-century: gangs of navy toughs armed with clubs and pistols roamed the port cities and the countryside miles inland, seizing able-bodied men walking down the street, working in the fields. These unlucky bastards, forcibly "recruited" on the spot, were dragged off to serve in the navy—often to their doom. Those who refused were beaten insensate and taken anyway.)

With England's finger hovering over the trigger, with Haddock cruising the Mediterranean ready to strike, and Brown on his way to the Jamaica Station, Walpole himself stepped in to take control of the flagging negotiations with Spain. The presence of Haddock's squadron in Spanish waters was now said to be causing Queen Isabela the sort of night terrors usually reserved for her husband. For her, this war seemed like "the Big One," with the fate of Spain's overseas empire at stake. Negotiations to avoid war on the part of Spain suddenly moved forward with renewed vigor. Spain had been building coastal fortifications; she now turned her full attention to diplomatic solutions. At last, in October 1738, with the help of the

Spanish ambassador to London, Don Geraldino, Spain and Britain reached a workable compromise.

Negotiations dragged into January 1739, through the drafting of proposals and counterproposals, the ironing out of details. At last, on January 27, Keene and la Quadra signed an agreement that came to be known as the Convention of El Pardo, named after the palace in Madrid where the negotiations and signing took place. In this document, Spain agreed to satisfy all outstanding British claims against the *guarda costas*, up to December 1737, for a total of £95,000, to be paid out in full within four months. Walpole breathed a sigh of relief. The Great Man had prevailed, saved his ministry from the opposition, and war had been averted. He immediately instructed the Admiralty to send orders to Haddock to cease his cruising and return home. Spain, anticipating war, had been meanwhile desperately building up her navy; as a gesture of conciliation, la Quadra ordered ship builders to back off from any new construction.

"They have unarmed the greater part of their Ships," Keene, now jubilant, wrote to Newcastle, "given liberty to their Officers to leave their Regiments and their Destinations."

The Convention of El Pardo had seemingly disposed of the immediate causes for war—compensation for British ships and cargo seized by *guarda costas*—but there remained three other important issues, as yet unresolved: 1) The British colony of Georgia, recently established for the benefit of "sturdy debtors" by the redoubtable James Oglethorpe on land la Quadra insisted—rightly—that by treaty belonged to Spain ("I fancy," Newcastle commented, regarding Spanish claims, "however the right may be it will now be pretty difficult to give up Georgia"); 2) British logging in what had become a de-facto British colony in Campeachy Bay—later called British Honduras, now Belize; and 3) the inalienable right to "Free Navigation," for British shipping in West Indian waters and elsewhere. This last matter was nonnegotiable: The chant of "No

Search! No Seizure!" had become the rallying cry of the London mobs. But none of these nuts were too tough for the nutcracker of diplomacy, so Keene believed. All would soon be settled by a comprehensive treaty to which the Convention of El Pardo was merely a preamble.

War averted for the moment, negotiations now entered a second phase: what would the new treaty look like? Inevitably, everything began to slow down. The diplomats quibbled. la Quadra remained stubborn; his colleague Montijo conciliatory. But even this comparatively mild-mannered gentleman could not stomach the rampant smuggling which had brought both nations to the brink of war.

"What would it avail if we should hang up a dozen of our Governors in America to please You," Keene reports Montijo complaining bitterly, "if you, the English, do not treat your Contrabandists with equal Rigour; You only hear of your Ships being taken, but you give no attention to the damages we suffer by Interlopers." In the same letter to Newcastle, the ambassador explains the situation further: "Besides, My Lord, no one who has any experience of this Court will ever believe they will come to any solid agreement, or any favorable extension of the American Treaty on their side, if they have not some apparent condescension on ours. The art and Difficulty will be to know when to yield, in order to get an advantageous Bargain."

Keene knew a reasonable compromise regarding smuggling and interdiction would ensure the success of the proposed treaty; Newcastle concurred. Articles detailing a plan to suppress illegal trade drawn up by Keene and his Spanish counterpart, the Marquis de Castres reached Newcastle on May 19, 1738. Their plan would include close supervision of all West Indian private traders (men like Jenkins and the shipowners out of Glasgow he worked for) but did not include in this scrutiny any vessels owned by the South Sea Company. Too many government officials, courtiers and indeed